# prefab green

# prefab green

Michelle Kaufmann / Catherine Remick

**GIBBS SMITH**
TO ENRICH AND INSPIRE HUMANKIND
Salt Lake City | Charleston | Santa Fe | Santa Barbara

First Edition
13 12 11 10 09    5 4 3 2 1

The project names of Michelle Kaufmann Designs used throughout
this book (Glidehouse, Breezehouse, mkSolaire, mkLotus, mkCustom,
mkPure, mkIsland, mkVessel, SolTerra, mkHearth, and SideBreeze) are
trademarked and owned by Michelle Kaufmann Designs.

Published by
Gibbs Smith
P.O. Box 667
Layton, Utah 84041

Orders: 1.800.835.4993
www.gibbs-smith.com

Designed by Catherine Remick
Produced by The Book Designers
www.bookdesigners.com
Printed and bound in China
Gibbs Smith books are printed on either recycled,
100% post-consumer waste, or FSC-certified papers.

Library of Congress Cataloging-in-Publication Data

Kaufmann, Michelle.
Prefab green / Michelle Kaufmann and Catherine Remick.—1st ed.
p. cm.
Includes bibliographical references.
ISBN-13: 978-1-4236-0497-6
ISBN-10: 1-4236-0497-0
1. Prefabricated houses. 2. Modular coordination (Architecture)
3. Sustainable design. I. Remick, Catherine. II. Title.
NA7145.K38 2009
728'.047—dc22
2008029258

To all who are dedicated to making this world a more beautiful place
now and for generations to come

The Sunset Breezehouse.

# Foreword

"If you can't find it, design it" is the long-standing and irresistible motto of Massimo and Leila Vignelli, those iconic designers of everything from Heller plastic melamine plates to the New York subway map. And it was perhaps the subconscious force compelling architect Michelle Kaufmann to create her first Glidehouse. This now near-seminal building, her first venture into modern green prefab, was borne out of Kaufmann's own unfulfilling search for a home of her own. She couldn't find it, so she designed it.

But she did so much more than that. Consider the term *modern green prefab*. It's rare to find a trio of such misconstrued, misunderstood, overused concepts. But with Kaufmann's elegant and practical designs, she creates the gold standard for the housing type. Stepping through the door of one of her homes silences any tired conversations about the coldness or inaccessibility of modernism, dispels any tree-hugging hippie clichés about the ugliness of sustainability, disproves the argument that solar is technologically or financially out of reach, and deftly illustrates that the pervasive stigma of prefab as cookie-cutter sameness is way out of date.

Now, nearly a decade into her exploration of the possibilities of green factory-built homes, Kaufmann has become a leading-edge figure of what is often called the "prefab movement." She has succeeded, I think, because of an unquestionable passion for the cause but also because of an unparalleled spirit of warmth and generosity that infuses equally her designs and her relationships with both clients and colleagues.

Michelle Kaufmann Designs is ever-evolving: new clients, new sites, new conditions continually give birth to new forms and ideas—the Glidehouse, Breezehouse, mkSolaire, mkLotus, mkLoft, and the SideBreeze. With each new iteration, she's not just expanded her market but contributed to the growth of a community, one that values not just the principles inherent in her designs but the intoxicating spirit with which they are executed.

—Allison Arieff
Editor-at-Large for *Sunset* Magazine, former Editor-in-Chief of *Dwell* magazine, and blog author for the *New York Times*

When I first met Michelle Kaufmann, in the fall of 2003, I was the Home Editor of *Sunset*, the West's largest and oldest lifestyle magazine. *Sunset* staffer Ann Castro had gotten me thinking about prefabs by putting a small news clipping from the *New York Times* on my desk. It talked about architects from the Midwest and East who were rethinking modular housing and made me wonder if anyone in the West had completed a modern prefab we could report. So I called Marshall Mayer, who was listed in the article as a western source for prefab news through his Web site livemodern.com. He referred me to Michelle, saying she had worked for Frank Gehry, had just moved to the Bay Area from Los Angeles, and was developing a great new prefab. I called her immediately, and she told me about the Glidehouse she and Kevin were building and the fact that she had really designed it to be factory built, and e-mailed me the plans and elevations.

I was captivated by its uncluttered outdoor-oriented design: the crisp shed roofs, elongated barn door screens along the front, and deceptively simple layout around a storage spine. The clarity, openness, and green factory-built nature of the Glidehouse seemed particularly appropriate for California and the West, like an update of a project from the Case Study Houses Program of the 1950s or a reinvention of the Eichler tract house from the same period, both of which were based on the concept of prefabrication but not fully realized. As *Sunset* wrote in 1978 (before my time): "The factory-built house has been a dream about to come true since the end of World War II." I thought the Glidehouse might be the start of the next chapter in the prefab saga, or at least be a good story, since it shared so much design DNA with what we had published in the 1950s and '60s.

At the same time, *Sunset*'s Marketing Director, Beth Whiteley, was looking for a significant new draw to the company's annual spring lifestyle festival called Celebration Weekend, when the company's twelve-acre Menlo Park headquarters opens to the general public for cooking, gardening, home décor, travel demonstrations, and even craft-making and wine-tasting. Her husband, Peter Whiteley, *Sunset*'s Senior Home Writer and overall building expert, had put up a hugely successful cabin the previous year, so she was looking for a sequel. When I told Beth about the Glidehouse, she immediately suggested that we debut it at CW in Sunset's parking lot. Michelle put us in touch with the company overseeing her first factory-built unit, and they in turn found a buyer. Construction, at a factory in British Columbia, took nineteen days. Then it was trucked in two sections down to Sunset, where buttoning up work and the building of an expansive deck designed by Peter Whiteley took about a week. Cliff May, the designer of Sunset's distinctive low-slung, garden-oriented building, would have been especially pleased, recognizing the Glidehouse as a descendant of the suburban ranch house, which he did so much to reinvent and popularize.

After advance press in the *New York Times* and other publications, the Glidehouse opened the following May to record crowds. As *Sunset* described it afterward: "It could have been the premiere of a summer blockbuster. The line to tour the Glidehouse . . . snaked out of sight. People waited for as long as an hour to get inside, which didn't stop one man from touring it six times. One person said: 'I liked the design so much I wanted to go home, burn my house down, and start over.'" The two-day event attracted a record-breaking crowd of nearly 25,000 visitors. We were ecstatic but also in shock. The rest, as they say, is prefab history.

The Glidehouse tapped a deep well of pent-up demand for fresh, contemporary, and affordable semi-custom home design. And it was just the beginning. The next year Michelle collaborated with us on the H-shaped Sunset Breezehouse, which was a contemporary adaptation of the dogtrot, with window walls that slide away to unite inside and outside in a continuous sweep of space. Once again a modern prefab was the star of the show. As this book shows, many more designs have followed. To paraphrase Frank Lloyd Wright, Michelle just seems to shake them out of her sleeve.

The finely tuned engine of innovation that is the Kaufmann firm has zoomed from zero to sixty in what seems like mere seconds, turning the dream of the imaginative, eco-friendly, cost-efficient factory-built house into reality. Where to next, Michelle? Let's go!

—Daniel P. Gregory
Editor-in-Chief, Houseplans.com
and author of *Cliff May and the Modern Ranch House*

The Kaufmann-Cullen Glidehouse.

# Introduction
## Dreaming of Green

As a child in Iowa, green was never more than a color, and sustainability (with its many meanings) was not a word used often. These terms were not a part of the Iowan dialect, but their connotations were at the root of the place and its culture. Iowa's farming industry dominates the economy. If farmers are having a good year, Iowans are basically happy. But during years of hardship and poor crops, everyone feels the farmers' suffering and hardship. Meet any person on the street, from friends to family or even strangers, and conversation typically begins with an assessment of the weather as it relates to the farmers: "Crops sure could use some rain," or "This early frost is trouble." Everyday acts of human community interact with the land and weather. The importance of the sensitive balance between man, nature, and climate has been ingrained in my consciousness since childhood.

However, I would later discover the supposed Midwest balance I observed as a child was not what it seemed. With its relatively low population density, Iowa never betrayed the realities of consumption and waste but rather hid them through the grand scale of its land and sky. When I moved to Princeton for graduate school and began spending time in New York, I realized how far from balanced our daily life had become. Maneuvering around masses of waste on dirty, congested New York streets was a wake-up call. Later, when I moved to Los Angeles, the impact of our oil addiction was all around me in the form of thick hovering smog. There were days it was difficult to even breathe!

The more I paid attention, the more I was convinced that our society was out of balance. But what could I do? Surely one person, one more car amidst the thousands clogging the 405 Freeway, could never do anything to restore the balance.

Although I was a graduate of a fine architecture school, I had not been formally introduced to the term *green building*. It wasn't until my husband, Kevin, and I began looking for a home of our own did I come to understand the true meaning of it.

Before embarking on our new-home search, we defined the characteristics we desired. We wanted a well-designed home with clean uncluttered spaces. We needed the home to produce low energy bills since we were on a budget (and we weren't about to give up Friday night sushi). After an awful experience with mold and headaches in our old rental house, we needed the home to possess healthy indoor air quality.

We also required a home made from low-maintenance materials. With both of us working long hours, we didn't have much time to spend on maintenance and improvements. We wanted our home to be made from materials we could feel good about that did not contribute to the destruction of the rainforests or an increase in carbon dioxide in the environment. Finally, we needed a home that fit into our budget . . . gulp. We soon learned our budget was unfit for homes on even the low end of the market. We could afford "teardowns," but if we followed that route, we wouldn't have any money left over to build anything. A home that possessed all the characteristics we were looking for simply did not exist in the Bay Area market at that time.

I believe we drove our real estate agent to the brink of madness. She believed our dream house list was way too long, completely unrealistic, and just plain making her job impossible. So, as a courtesy, we condensed it to "clean and green" and (fingers crossed) within our budget. Even with our pared-down requirements, nothing was available. But we soldiered on.

We spent an excruciating six months attending every open house we could find. Every Sunday and Tuesday I would diligently map out a precise plan for us to pursue—five home visits in a four-hour period. Each morning as I laid out the day's plan, I remained ridiculously optimistic: surely today would be the day we would find our home! At the end of each day, however, Kevin and I would recap our findings. This usually ended in my desperate attempt to come up with reasons why a foul-smelling unsuitable home that required us to walk through the bathroom to access the bedroom could quite possibly be our dream house. We could make it work!

I was getting drawn into the frenzied madness of the real estate world. I would think, "We have to move fast because this opportunity won't last!" Clearly, I was becoming way too emotionally invested in our home search. My capacity for logical thought was evaporating as quickly as homes were being snapped up off the market. Fortunately, Kevin was able to maintain his grip on reality. He gently pointed out that even if we truly believed we could live with the curry-smelling, pink-tiled kitchen or the drafty single-pane windows, it was all still out of our price range. How could this be?

I had to face facts. The home we wanted did not exist, and no amount of wishing would make it so. We weren't bad people or reaping some karma, and it was pointless to wallow in self-pity. We felt propelled into action—we had to live *somewhere*. Our solution was to build something for ourselves. Initially, I wondered why we hadn't thought of this before—I'm an architect; Kevin is a talented cabinet, furniture, and stair builder—perfect! My naivety turned out to be a blessing.

Unable to find an affordable, well-designed, sustainable home, we decided to create our own. We purchased a narrow lot in a semirural city in Marin County, California, and began to plan for an efficient green dwelling with a thoughtful connection to the outdoors. The project moved at a quick pace as we worked to complete the design within the forty-five-day escrow period.

Kevin challenged me on every decision; he was always questioning, always pushing for greener solutions. Choosing materials that would draw the least from the earth's natural

"the Glidehouse" because of the sliding components—adjustable cedar sunshades, glass doors, and the unique sliding storage bar along the backs of the rooms. We designed our Glidehouse for climate, functionality, and environmentally responsible living. With the environment in mind, we chose structural insulated panels (SIPs), hoping to stay within budget and save time. SIPs have a place in green building, but they also have downsides and limitations. We continued building our home with SIPs but also started to research other options.

Intrigued by our unique home-construction project, friends

Unable to find an affordable, well-designed, sustainable home, we decided to create our own. We purchased a narrow lot in a semirural city in Marin County, California, and began to plan for an efficient green dwelling with a thoughtful connection to the outdoors.

resources and wouldn't require much maintenance over time were big priorities. We designed the house based not just on how it would look but also on how it would feel. By installing photovoltaic (PV) solar panels, the home would have a zero electric bill. We carefully planned the home to use less water, energy, and materials. We designed the home with a series of sliding glass doors, sliding wood panels, and sliding wood sunshades. We not only loved our new home, but it met every single goal we started out with.

We nicknamed our three-bedroom, 1,560-square-foot home

and colleagues asked if they could have a modern green house too. So I began researching mass production and working on parallel tracks. For our site, the most affordable approach was to use SIPs. But I was also researching how a factory could make our home and was finding maximum dimensions for shipping the modules on flatbed trucks. My persistence paid off when I found a prefab factory willing to give me a chance. Our site-built home took fourteen months to construct. The factory built an identical Glidehouse in four months at a cost 15 percent less than the site-built Glidehouse.

# Glidehouse Comparison

| | March 2003 | April | May | June | July | August | September | October |
|---|---|---|---|---|---|---|---|---|

**KAUFMANN-CULLEN GLIDEHOUSE (SITE BUILT)**

| Task | March 2003 | April | May | June | July | August | September | October |
|---|---|---|---|---|---|---|---|---|
| FINDING A SITE FOR THE HOUSE | ███ | | | | | | | |
| DESIGN / SCHEMATIC DRAWINGS | | ███ | | | | | | |
| ARCH / STRUCTURAL AND ENGINEERING DRAWINGS | | ████████████ | | | | | | |
| PERMIT PROCESS | | | | | ██████████████ | | | |
| SUBCONTRACTOR BID PROCESS | | | | | | ████████ | | |
| FOUNDATION / SITE WORK | | | | | | | | |
| CONSTRUCTION OF HOUSE | | | | | | | | |
| FINAL PAYMENT W/ CONSTRUCTION LOAN | | | | | | | | |
| MOVE-IN DATE | | | | | | | | |

**ANDREW/KINDRA REID GLIDEHOUSE (MODULAR)**

| Task | March 2003 | April | May | June | July | August | September | October |
|---|---|---|---|---|---|---|---|---|
| FINDING A SITE FOR THE HOUSE | | | | | | | | |
| ARCH / STRUCTURAL AND ENGINEERING DRAWINGS | | | | | | | | |
| PERMIT PROCESS | | | | | | | | |
| FACTORY PRICING | | | | | | | | |
| FOUNDATION / SITE WORK | | | | | | | | |
| CONSTRUCTION OF THE HOUSE | | | | | | | | |
| SHIPPING / SETTING | | | | | | | | |
| FINAL PAYMENT | | | | | | | | |
| MOVE-IN DATE | | | | | | | | |

November | December | **January 2004** | February | March | April | May | June | July | August | September | October | November | December

After our challenging experience, I realized something extremely important: my earlier belief that I could not make a difference was simply untrue. My idle thought process only made it easier for me to consume resources without consideration for the impact I was having on the planet. Every day, every one of us has the power to make choices that will result in less usage and less waste. Individually, each person can make a difference in this world; collectively, we can save it.

In the years since building our home, I have discovered that many people feel the same way Kevin and I did. People are desperately trying to find healthy, green, efficient homes for their families. Most importantly, they care about the environment and their children's future. However, the information and solutions are not always easy to find. People are uncertain of what to do and the best way to do it. People are busy, people have budgets, and people want simplicity. Where are the easy, affordable green solutions?

I had some awareness and understanding of prefab construction, but during our building process, my interest grew. One reason for this was the important book by Allison Arieff and Bryan Burkhart, *Prefab*. Through her work with *Dwell* magazine and the book, Allison had single-handedly made *prefab* a word that once again embodied the goal of good design for the masses. After decades of being viewed as substandard trailer homes, prefab was now synonymous with high design. I also credit my sage friend Ryan Stevens. As I laid my head in exasperation on the counter at one of our favorite pubs, recounting my latest frustrations over house hunting, Ryan whispered, "Prefab. You should look into it. Maybe that is your answer."

Here, SIPs panels are placed on the original Glidehouse.

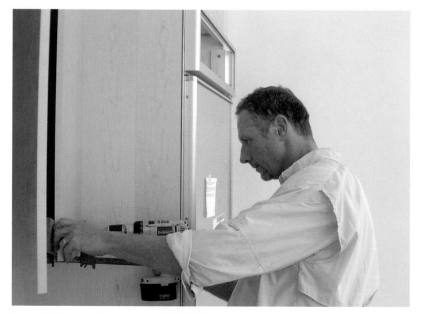

Kevin Cullen working on the first Glidehouse.

In fact, the home Kevin and I built was prefabricated in a small way. We used SIPs (structural insulated panel system) for the walls, floors, and roofs. These panels had been precision cut off-site and shipped on a truck to our site. The literature accompanying the SIPs panels had promised less time, less money, and higher insulation value. While the insulation was more energy efficient than other insulation options, using these panels for our home did not cost less or minimize time. Upon reflection, however, the results might have been different in a mass-production or more repetitive setting.

As I contemplated making our house in mass production, I investigated different prefabrication techniques. I found that *modular* factories offer the potential for high-quality design, precision cutting, less waste, increased quality control, and short production time frames compared to the traditional site-built process. This was the answer to my question. Yes, we could make our house in mass production and, as a result, we could significantly reduce waste, maximize material efficiency, and decrease oil usage. We could offer our Glidehouse design so that others could have a reasonably affordable green home while avoiding the painful process that Kevin and I experienced.

And that was the beginning of Michelle Kaufmann Designs, which I founded soon after as an architectural practice working only in green modular designs. I began this firm to create thoughtful sustainable design and to make it more accessible for everyone. Sustainable healthy living should be for everybody.

Designers and builders need to lead the way and make environmentally friendly design easy and affordable. We need to

Michelle working on her home, watering the home's cor-ten steel siding.

The completed Kaufmann-Cullen Glidehouse.

rethink how we work and how we build, and let sustainability be our guide. We must think deeply about our designs but execute and install them simply, without waste and without damage to the land. The following chapters describe our path to this goal of making it easy and beautiful to go green.

—Michelle Kaufmann

Indoor and outdoor spaces combine in the original Glidehouse.

The library of a Sunset Breezehouse.

*"Everybody wants the same thing, rich or poor . . .
not only a warm, dry room, but a shelter for the soul."*

—SAMUEL MOCKBEE

## Thoughtful Sustainable Design for Everyone

When I embarked on the work I do now, I wasn't thinking like an architect. I was just another renter in search of a decent home to buy. As an average middle-class professional in the San Francisco Bay Area, I assumed that with enough patience and searching, I would be able to find a modest affordable home.

Was I ever wrong. After walking through a seemingly endless array of overpriced uninspiring houses, I began to realize that the architecture profession had largely overlooked the needs of the average aspiring homeowner like me. Architect-designed personalized homes can be miniature masterpieces, of course, but they are rarely affordable for anyone but the most affluent. As well, most architecture firms focus their energies on designing skyscrapers, museums, and other civic structures; thus the job of creating functional well-designed housing for average families has largely become the business of the building industry. Although the industry has done a good job of meeting consumer demand, these homes, which are often large and poorly designed, are not always beautiful and inspiring.

Rather than complain about landscapes filled with oversized uninspiring homes, I resolved to do something about it. Why couldn't we rethink the concept of a home? After all, our homes are the buildings where we spend most of our time. They are the places where we raise our families, where we retreat from the outside world to relax and socialize with friends, and where we can express our own tastes and style—why should they be lackluster and even unhealthy? Like me, most people want homes that are affordable, enduring, healthy, and—now more than ever—environmentally sound.

I made it my goal to marry good design with minimal environmental impact to create "green" homes that would be available to everyone. To do this, I had to create an uncomplicated system that would use the principles of mass production to blend sustainable home layouts, eco-friendly materials, and low-energy options to create a "prepackaged" green solution to home design. A few architect friends of mine expressed skepticism about the viability of such a mass production endeavor. As they pointed out, many architects before me had tried (some more successfully than others) to design prefab structures for the masses. Others warned that promoting design for the masses might lead other architects to view me as "selling out." But I strongly believe that architecture is a service, one that shouldn't be available only to the wealthy or highly educated. Good design can and should make life better and more beautiful for everyone.

I soon realized that I would have to start thinking less like an architect and more like a product designer. As I began researching the history of mass production and product design, I was delighted to realize that I was following in the footsteps of other architects who had successfully created great design for minimal cost, largely by making use of standardized parts. Charles and Ray Eames, for example, the legendary American designers in the 1940s to the 1970s, were best known for their work in architecture, furniture design, industrial design, and manufacturing. The Eameses' unique vision was to bring "the good life" to the general public through modern materials, new technologies, and high-quality design. To do this, they promoted mass production of their furniture and architectural elements. Their groundbreaking work included the iconic Eames Chair and their Case Study House in Pacific Palisades, California—widely considered to be one of the

Charles and Ray Eames.

The Eames Case Study House.

most important postwar residences ever built. I was greatly encouraged by their firm belief that design—big or small—could improve people's lives.

I also explored the work of Joseph Eichler, a revolutionary developer from the 1950s, who redefined suburbia by teaming up with architects such as Quincy Jones to create affordable, progressive home designs. Between 1949 and 1974,

Eichler built 11,000 unique homes using mainly prefab parts, providing much-needed housing for the 1950s middle class. Today, Eichler's pioneering homes are still beautiful, modern, enduring masterpieces. With efficient, open floor plans and light-filled atriums, the homes feel as fresh and innovative today as they did fifty years ago.

I also drew inspiration from the work of my mentors Michael Graves and Frank Gehry, two of contemporary architecture's most remarkable practitioners. Although best known for their stunning building designs, both Graves and Gehry are also product designers. Michael Graves was one of the first contemporary architects to venture beyond the realm of building design into product design. The teakettle he designed for Alessi, a playful and beautiful re-creation of the standard kitchen kettle, quickly became a modern icon and quieted the criticism of other architects who had cynically predicted failure for his product designs. Today Graves has branched out to design home furnishings, jewelry, and dinnerware for

An Eichler home.

A light-filled Eichler interior.

companies such as Disney, Steuben, Phillips Electronics, and Black & Decker. More recently, he teamed up with Target retail stores to create many beautiful affordable products that remain some of the store's most popular housewares. Frank Gehry's signature sinuous style of architecture can also be found in objects other than his buildings. He has designed a number of lines of jewelry for Tiffany & Co. and has worked with other companies, including Knoll and Swatch, to design furniture, light fixtures, housewares, and watches.

With these inspirations in mind, I decided to pursue the creation of mass-produced sustainable homes. I founded Michelle Kaufmann Designs (MKD) in 2002, with only a few employees. In what I like to call "Version 1.0" of the firm, we were a classic architectural practice, specializing in modular construction. The four of us—myself, Dick Hawkinson, Scott Landry, and Paul Warner, quickly learned to navigate the often-challenging terrain of acquiring permits and construction documents, and we became adept multitaskers. The early days were exciting and frenzied—we did everything ourselves and really stretched the boundaries of what it meant to be an architect. We were engaged in construction, education, marketing, product design, and factory science. We eventually created flexible models and nimble construction methods to meet the needs of individual clients.

At the same time MKD Version 1.0 was forming, broader public interest in prefab design was growing. Spurred by home and lifestyle magazines such as *Sunset* and *Dwell,* the general public began to consider the many benefits of preassembled

design. Allison Arieff, former editor-in-chief of *Dwell* magazine and coauthor of the book *Prefab,* spearheaded the *Dwell* Home competition, which demonstrated the varied ways prefab could be well designed, beautiful, and sustainable.

Similarly, Michael Sylvester's innovative Web site, www.fabprefab.com, offers an online community for designers and prefab companies to meet to compare notes on their experiences. The Web site is stocked with information for people interested in learning more about prefabrication, and it has become an effective way for potential clients to reach prefab designers. For example, on the day we posted our initial Glidehouse renderings to the site, we received two inquiries for purchase. More questions and orders poured in over the next few days. We eventually relied on another online community creator, Marshall Mayer of www.livemodern.com to start responding to e-mails and answering the questions of potential clients.

We also benefitted greatly from Dan Gregory, Beth Whiteley, and Peter Whiteley of *Sunset* magazine. Their wonderful ideas and generous spirit were instrumental in the success of MKD. The Glidehouse debut at *Sunset* magazine's Celebration Weekend provided much-needed exposure to our modest start-up at a critical time. And their unending support, articles, and advice were so helpful.

The conventional wisdom among architects holds that although prefab design is a wonderful idea in theory, it is nearly impossible to make it succeed in practice. I disagree. The skepticism about prefab design stems in part from the

Outdoor rooms and the sliding barn-door
sunscreen of a Glidehouse.

negative experiences people have had with prefab during the past two decades. But circumstances have changed dramatically since then, not least in how we communicate with and educate the public. The Internet has revolutionized the way we do business. Web communities (like Sylvester's Fabprefab) offer advantages to designers and clients that were unimaginable just a few years ago. We can collaborate with other designers irrespective of location. And we can build business relationships all over the world without having to fly to distant locations or wait for the postal service to deliver a letter.

Naturally, at MKD we like to meet our clients face to face for our first few meetings, but once the process has begun, we communicate via e-mail and a shared online server. We quickly and easily update drawings and exchange ideas with clients. Unlike architectural practice twenty years ago, we don't need to meet in person to review every drawing or selection. We also have computerized technology like Google's Sketchup and CAD that allow us to produce, edit, and customize homes quickly and accurately. New technologies also give us the power to merge sustainable design with efficient mass production.

Although prefabrication and mass production can save time and sometimes money, it has to be intelligent and thoughtful. No one wants to live in a generic box of a house that fails to respect a particular site's climate or orientation. I recognize the importance of working closely with clients to create a home that is uniquely in harmony with its surroundings. Our homes need to meet the individual needs of the people who live in them. This is the kind of architecture that energizes me—homes that are economical to build and operate, that serve the people who live in them, and that don't take too much from the earth.

MKD has evolved over the years. On a day I will never forget, one of my partners, Joseph Remick, called me out of the blue and said, "We really need our own factory." I agreed completely, but the thought of locating a factory and getting it up and running was daunting in light of the other work we had to do. Later that same day, I received a phone call from Marty Moore, our shipping guru. He told me about a man, Harold Hansen, who was nearing retirement and wanted to sell his modular home factory. I took this as a sign it was meant to be, and we purchased the factory, giving us control over the manufacturing process. MKD now builds many of our own designs, an infrequent occurrence in the architecture field.

At the same time we purchased the factory, we shored up additional factory partners to meet demand and started a new contract process. Recent developments in manufacturing and materials coupled with the innovative talents of new employees helped us immensely. In addition to hiring talented designers and architects, we also focused on hiring from outside the architecture profession. New team members included CEOs, vice presidents, and project managers from companies such as Autodesk, Hewlitt Packard, GE, and Gehry Technologies. We also brought on John Mick, who specializes in automation in building construction and plant design. Lisa Gansky, an experienced brand and operations genius, rounds out the MKD team. A conventional architecture firm does not typically employ such a diverse range of people. But in order to maximize efficiency at every step of the production and distribution process, we transformed ourselves into something beyond an architecture firm—a mix of architecture, product design, and construction.

With the help of Michael Sylvester, we created a streamlined six-step process to guide clients toward home ownership. Purchasing land and then designing and building a home on it can be daunting to new clients. Our efficient six-step method combines elements of both architecture and product design to simplify the client experience.

We now offer three separate categories of home: preconfigured, custom, and communities. Preconfigured homes are the original models of our modular homes and are within reach financially for most homeowners. Clients choose finishes from a catalog of preselected options and enjoy a shortened design and engineering time frame. With predictable costs, shortened construction time, and reduced design fees, preconfigured homes are efficient yet contain all the green amenities and artistic elements of an architect-designed home.

The customized home is our second category. Customization is easily accomplished with factory construction, allowing clients to pay a bit more to create a custom design, add additional space, or incorporate higher-end materials. Custom homes still utilize off-site technology and have the benefit of sustainable materials, shortened time frames, and cost predictability.

The communities category we are particularly excited about focuses on multifamily dwellings, hotels, resorts, and educational facilities. Developers are starting to realize the many advantages of prefabricated architecture. Shorter time frames, predictable costs, and lowered risks and liabilities are only a few of the benefits associated with off-site modular technology. Through the use of smart sustainable design and site strategies, energy-efficient systems, and eco-friendly materials, we create communities that are healthy, beautiful, and cost effective. We believe this housing category holds the most promise for affordability, reach, and impact.

In addition to homes and communities, MKD is also creating green products on a smaller scale. For example, our Vessel light fixture is elegant, simple, and energy efficient. The mkPure concrete sink, made from concrete infused with fly ash, recycled porcelain, or rice hull, provides a stylish and earth-friendly alternative to the conventional bathroom sink. And the mkIsland combines the beauty of a concrete-topped kitchen island with the functionality of a table. This flexible multiuse piece saves space and complements any kitchen.

A less tangible but no less important green idea we have been embracing is "eco-luxury." Eco-luxury is not about climbing out of your lavish high-thread-count organic cotton sheets, washing your face with decadent all-natural beauty products, and then jumping into your expensive, designer biodegradable shirt to make a stylish statement. It is not green consumerism. Instead, we are asserting the idea that sustainable living does not need to be uncomfortable and barren. Incorporating sustainable practices and solutions into your life does not mean a drab unfulfilled life devoid of beauty.

The definition of "luxury" in the more traditional sense implies something that is expensive, hard to attain, and not needed. We believe the concept of luxury can be redefined as something more reachable to the average person. Eco-luxury is about the quality of your lifestyle more than the quantity of material goods in it. Natural gifts such as clean air, good light, refreshing breezes, and beautiful views are at the heart of this idea. These luxuries should not only be accessible to the privileged but should be a part of everyone's life. Everybody should experience the joy of living in a home that provides high-quality air, natural light, freshness, and simple beauty. A sense of luxury can be derived from a clean healthful lifestyle.

Our team is working diligently to streamline the home design and building process so that green prefab homes can reach the mass market. Everyone should enjoy the luxuries of a clean, healthy, beautiful lifestyle. By combining function with beauty, we offer clients a superior experience, both physically and emotionally, in their homes. We are committed to continuing to offer new ideas for the next generation of housing, and look forward to seeing more people living happily in their well-designed, healthy, and sustainable homes.

The "Smart + Wired" mkSolaire at the Chicago Museum of Science + Industry.

This Sunset Breezehouse in Sonoma, California, utilizes the latest green technologies to minimize its impact on the environment.

*There are no small gestures when it comes to going green; every change you make in the way you live and interact with the environment can help make the world a better place.*

## The Five EcoPrinciples

Hear the phrase *global warming,* and the images that pop into your mind's eye are most likely of your car's tailpipe or an airplane's wing engine or a factory's smokestack. You probably don't conjure a vision of the quarter-inch gap under your back door, the length of pipe running from your water heater to your shower, or the type of wood your framing is made from. But considering the fact that buildings in the United States account for 38 percent of our total carbon emissions, maybe you should. Buildings are responsible for a larger percentage of the United State's total emissions than transportation. Buildings are also the biggest energy consumers in the country. They consume 40 percent of the total energy and claim 70 percent of total electricity usage.

The impact of buildings extends even beyond energy usage and emissions. As discussion grows around the topic of the decreasing availability of freshwater on our planet (and the associated threats), we should remember that buildings in the

United States are using 25 percent of the total amount of water consumed here and producing 20 percent of water effluents. As natural resources and clean habitats grow more scarce—our forests are disappearing, oil reserves are drying up, islands of plastic are growing in our oceans—buildings in this country are taking up 30 percent of the total raw materials used here and 25 percent of solid waste created.

These are discouraging facts. However, there is good news that comes from all this: because buildings have such an impact on our environment, designers and builders can make an enormous positive impact on the planet through the choices made in our work. If we choose materials and systems that use less energy and resources, then we can be a powerful ally in the global battle to reduce carbon emissions and other damage. We need to start thinking outside the traditional parameters that lead us to prefer what is cheapest and fastest. We should think in more holistic terms of what

A detail of a Glidehouse sliding sunshade.

environmental costs, not just monetary, will be incurred through our decisions. We must also put a premium on longevity. Home dwellers can make a big difference as well. A sustainable approach to building a home not only provides the healthiest living space possible but also makes it easier for you to minimize your negative impact on the environment.

So what exactly is sustainable design? As more and more companies are coming out with "green" and "sustainable" products, it can all get a bit confusing. Opinions vary on the best ways to create a sustainable environment, and in the end you need to decide what works best for your life. We have developed the five EcoPrinciples, which offer an organized way of looking at and understanding ways to go green.

When designing homes and products, we consider and create sustainable design based on these EcoPrinciples: smart design, eco-materials, energy efficiency, water conservation,

Low-maintenance cor-ten steel siding on a Glidehouse is reflected in the home's rainwater catchment system.

and healthy environment. We believe so strongly in each of these principles that we implement every one of them into our designs. The wonderful thing about these principles is their ability to be introduced into any new or existing home or building. You have the power to incorporate some or all of them into your life, depending on your particular budget and living situation.

## Smart Design

Perhaps the most essential of the five EcoPrinciples is the first: smart design. A house that begins with smart design can sustain a low impact on the environment throughout its lifetime. Smart design is the fundamental design of a building—creating a foundation for sustainability. Smart decisions during the design process (layout of the floor plan, the positioning of windows and doors, and the very orientation of the house) can make green living easier and more successful. While smart design does not cost any more than the traditional approach to building, it is more likely to save money over the long term. Most importantly, smart design is thoughtful and will add greater beauty to your day-to-day life. The following eleven smart design elements are excellent ways to ensure that a space is created using minimal resources.

### Design to Use Less

Of course, the most sustainable material is the one we don't use. But human beings tend to prefer indoor living to total exposure. We have a need to exist within an enclosed space

for security and to protect ourselves against the elements. Using materials and other natural resources to build our dwellings is unavoidable. Still, we should take every step possible to reduce the amount of material and natural resources that go into the construction and maintenance of our homes.

### Design Big, Don't Build Big

Designing big instead of building big is an essential element of smart design and one we strongly believe in. With proper care, you can make a space feel larger than it is and maximize its utility so more square footage is unnecessary. By building only what is needed and sizing rooms correctly, we can reduce the impact a structure has on the environment. We must begin to free ourselves from the notion that "bigger is better" and realize that better is better, regardless of size.

Between 1950 and 2004, the average American living space tripled from an average of 290 square feet per person to 900 square feet per person. What was sufficient space for a house in 1950 is now only a third of the size of our current homes. This is odd considering humans feel more comfortable in properly scaled, cozy rooms rather than oversized ones. Yet so many current homes are enormous in proportion to our human bodies. The homes are getting bigger and bigger while the quality of their design is getting worse and worse. Why?

One reason for the increasing size of houses in this country is that realtors and builders describe the price of a home in terms of cost per square foot. As homes get bigger, the cost per square foot decreases, but in order for a builder to still make a profit, certain cutbacks are made that diminish the quality of the home. Combine this drop in quality with the now overblown scope of the building and you have a space that no longer feels comfortable or in harmony with our bodies. In fact, some good friends of mine live in just such a house—one that is much too large for anything but parties. They do have great parties in their home, but for more intimate settings of four or five people, it just is not comfortable sitting in one of their huge rooms. We always gravitate toward the kitchen and end up chatting there because it is the one room that feels scaled to our bodies.

Aside from creating properly scaled living spaces, designing big rather than building big means you end up building less, as you might have guessed. Building less not only costs less from the onset but also saves money over the long term since there ends up being less space to heat in the winter and cool during the summer. Therefore, building less also lays the foundation for greater energy efficiency in a home.

Smart design can make a smaller space feel bigger in numerous ways. One of our favorite techniques is bringing the outdoors inside the home. With elements such as glass doors and connecting gardens, courtyards, and decks, you can extend the sense of space outside the walls of a house and into the surrounding environment. We can make a space feel larger than it is by, in effect, "borrowing" space from the outdoors. High ceilings are another wonderful design element that can make a space feel much larger. Taller spaces are also helpful

during the warmer months because hot air can rise up and out of the living space below.

**Design For Double Function**

Make one thing serve the purpose of two and you eliminate the need for the second. We should expect more out of each part, each item in our home. In the homes we design at MKD,

The mkSolaire uses roof decks and covered outdoor spaces to enlarge the home's usable area.

this idea has evolved beyond a simple sofa-bed concept. For example, in our Glidehouse we can extend the stone hearth at the foot of the fireplace out to the front door of the house so that it doubles as an entry vestibule. The kitchen in an mkLotus is illuminated naturally through a skylight (which is what a skylight is supposed to do), but we take it further and ensure the skylight is operable so hot air can escape, ventilating the room.

All this is not to say a sofa bed is not a great example of double function; it's a terrific piece of double-functioning furniture for an office or guest room. In fact, there are many ways to obtain more out of the furniture in a home. In my own Glidehouse living room, I just love the stools that double as mini storage spaces. I also love the creative storage solutions that my friends, the Remicks, have found in their Breezehouse: their bed lifts up to reveal a storage space below; their pantry is set deep with

outdoor rooms. This is an idea similar to what I mentioned earlier about bringing the outdoors inside as means for "designing big." In this case, you can actually expand your living space beyond the walls of your home. By designing the exterior spaces of a house as thoughtfully as the interior, you can extend your sense of space and embrace the environment in which you live.

Skylights not only bring in light but also ventilate a room.

The built-in cabinetry and clever under-bed storage allow for double functions.

pullout shelves, and they have invisible wall-mounted shelving for books that take up zero floor space. It is all so clever and very useful.

**Design Outdoor Rooms as Much as Indoor Rooms**

Another creative and very beautiful way to maximize the utility and function of a smaller space is by designing adjacent

This fairly inexpensive solution can also work during the very warm or very cold months when outdoor rooms are not used as often. Glass windows and walls can allow you to maintain that sense of extended outdoor space. Design elements such as overhead trellises and varying ground material are very effective in defining outdoor rooms.

## Design to Find Space on the Roof

A roof can do more than sit on top of a home and protect it. Roof decks, gardens, and green roofs are creative and beautiful ways to get the most out of a home. By maximizing the space on top of the home, every inch of the home is utilized. This is especially important with tighter lots, smaller houses, and more urban environments.

A roof deck, like the one on the MSI mkSolaire, can maximize space in an urban environment.

## Design to Keep Lights Off During the Day

With well-placed glass windows and doors, the need for lights during the daytime is eliminated. Windows and doors can be positioned to wash indoor surfaces with natural light in a well-balanced way. For example, the glass walls of the Glidehouse bathe the floors in light while high clerestory windows do the same to the ceilings, creating a balance.

The idea is not to randomly place a large amount of glass everywhere, which can create hot spots, heat gain, and glare, but rather to strategically place glass where it can do the most good. Punching windows into a wall provides light, but it also creates the opposite of light: darkness, or shadow. Faced with both, our eyes tire easily from trying to compensate for the contrast, and this is why we need lights on during the day. But when you wash a surface with light from well-placed windows, you can minimize contrast in a room, making artificial lighting unnecessary.

Skylights do a fantastic job of bringing more natural light into a space and reducing the need for artificial light. Skylights are tricky. You don't want to use too many or have them in the wrong places, creating solar heat gain. Solatubes, small cylinders with reflective interiors, are another option. These mini skylights maximize the natural light passing through but minimize the glare and heat gain normally associated with sunlight.

## Design to Heat and Cool Naturally

Another accomplishment of smart design is eliminating the need to artificially heat and cool a space. At MKD, we challenge the idea that adjusting the temperature in a home means touching the thermostat. We design a shallow footprint for our homes, which maximizes cross ventilation. Designing cross ventilation into a space allows fresh air to cool it during the hot summer months and also creates proper, healthy air exchange in the spring and fall. Adjustments to the indoor temperature can easily be made by simply opening or closing a window or sunshade.

### Design to Collaborate with the Landscape

A site-appropriate home that collaborates with the land is a major element of our smart design EcoPrinciple. We thoroughly analyze the site in order to reach a solution most fitting

Simply adjusting a sunshade can cool a room naturally.

to a home's lot. Climate, topography, and the cultural vernacular are all carefully considered. The following six basics must also be kept in mind when your goal is to design a building to work in concert with its landscape:

**Have a Small Impact on the Land**—At every turn, minimize the force a building will have on the land, both in terms of the impact of the built structure itself and also the techniques employed during its construction. Keeping the majority of the construction off-site by using prefabricated modular technology does a lot to protect the land on a site because it reduces the number of trucks and laborers on it, minimizing wear and tear. A key preventative measure is an adequate erosion-control plan in place before construction. The built structure should also incorporate proper grading and drainage design, reducing storm-water runoff and maintaining existing water drainage pathways.

**Connect with the Land**—Design the building to feel like it was always there, as if the home could only be present on that particular site. The building should be integrated to the site so that it exists in perfect harmony with the land and surroundings. The idea of doing more with less can apply to a site as easily as a building. Forming a connection with the land doesn't require a lot of acreage or a remote untouched site. By implementing good, thoughtful landscape design on even the smallest of lots, the building site can be transformed and every square inch of space maximized. Small gardens can be lovely places for contemplation, and they do a wonderful job of connecting the home to the outdoors.

**Remember Solar Orientation**—Proper solar orientation is crucial in reducing heat gain in a building. A north-south orientation with the majority of windows facing south is typically best. The number and size of windows facing westward should be minimized and require sun shading to prevent excessive heat gain in the afternoons. Sun-blocking solutions such as trellises, roof overhangs, louvers, sunshades, and vegetation should be designed to maximize the weak heat of the winter sun, which comes in low, and also to reduce the powerful heat of the summer afternoon sun, which comes in high.

**Make Use of the Views**—A balance must be struck between the best solar orientation for glass windows and doors and the views a site has to offer. Views of beautiful landscape elements, near and far, as well as views into and out of neighboring homes must be taken into account to marry aesthetic goals and privacy. One effective but underutilized solution is high clerestory windows. These wonderful windows bring light in from above, offer terrific views of trees and sky, facilitate cross ventilation, and provide privacy.

**Make Use of the Breezes**—Before building, analyze natural breeze patterns on the site. In extremely breezy areas, it is best to protect outdoor rooms from heavy winds. In hotter climates, orienting windows to capture breezes will offer better relief from the heat. High, centrally located ceilings and operable windows and walls help to produce a "chimney effect" in a room. This chimney effect is based on the natural tendency of air to move from high to low pressures (natural ventilation). The warm air naturally rises, causing air movement through

the home. The mkSolaire is a good example of a home designed to maximize this effect.

**Reduce the Effects of Grading**—Virtually every site requires some grading to help direct the flow of rainwater runoff away from the home, but there are techniques that reduce the impact it has on the land. Whenever a foundation is laid, there needs to be some excavation of the land; the steeper the slope of the site, the more excavation is needed, which also raises

A Glidehouse makes use of the view and breezes.

the cost of it. One way to mitigate the impact and cost of excavation is the cut-and-fill technique, which entails "cutting" the uphill soil that needs to be removed and then using it to "fill" in the downhill area that needs leveling. You essentially cut a stair into the hillside, shifting existing soil instead of removing it.

Another grading technique is the creation of earth berms around a structure. Berms are just fancy words for mounds of soil piled against the exterior of a building, but they are an effective way to control the slope of the ground and the flow of runoff water. By providing wind protection and insulation, berms are an especially beneficial and affordable solution for colder climates. Berms can be combined with thoughtful landscaping to beautifully nestle a structure into the land. No matter how you grade a site, by using minimal concrete and removing as little earth as possible, you can do a lot to lessen a building's initial impact on the land.

### Design for Longevity

Design something to last, particularly a home, and you'll be doing yourself, any future owners, and the planet a big favor. Longevity is an important part of smart design. The "here today, gone tomorrow" phenomenon we see with many consumer goods is so wasteful and has no place in the housing industry. A home should be designed to stand the test of time, and there are two very good ways of doing this.

Designing a home with low-maintenance, long-lasting materials (metal and stone) is the first way to create a lasting home. Exteriors such as painted sidings or wood (excluding a species like cedar that stands up very well to the elements) require a certain degree of upkeep over their lifetime, consuming time, money, and natural resources. However, if you employ a siding such as weathering steel, which is actually meant to rust and get stronger as it does, then you'll enjoy very little

maintenance. The second way to design for longevity is to ensure the home has a classic timeless design, immune to passing trends or fads that might need updating.

### Design for Flexibility

Flexibility is crucial if a home is to adapt to the growing and changing needs of a family. Flexibility is an essential element

Long-lasting materials such as cor-ten steel and cedar siding mean very little maintenance for this home.

of smart design in these two ways: flexibility in future use and flexibility in controls.

**Flexibility for Future Use**—One way we can create an adaptable home is to make it "future proof" with electronic systems and technology easily accessible for potential updates and advances. In fact, we are currently working on a "smart spine" approach to future flexibility. The spine, which runs the length of the home, carries the electrical and HVAC systems, and is easily accessed for updating and replacing.

Homes with strictly programmed single-use spaces are not flexible and cannot adjust if a family's needs change. Rooms and spaces must possess a certain amount of fluidity to flow from one intended use to another. A family's requirements evolve over time as children grow older and lifestyles change. With solutions like multiuse open spaces and sliding walls, we can achieve flexibility and expand the possibilities for each room.

We also like to plan for anticipated changes. For example, there is the prospect that the average family will not require storage for two automobiles in the future. Hopefully, the need will be mitigated through improvements and expansions to alternatives like mass public transit. So how do you transition a garage space? One answer we have developed within the mkSolaire is a garage adjacent to a landscaped living-space courtyard. With glass garage doors on both the front and the back of the space, the garage can transform into a wonderful studio, office, or playroom that opens to a garden space.

**Flexibility in Controls**—Unfortunately, important systems in a home such as light, temperature, and ventilation are usually designed in a "one size fits all" manner with little regard for individual preferences. If you get too cold in your bedroom at night, you have to heat the whole house. By designing flexibility into lighting and heating systems in your home, you can

control these elements according to your preferences for maximum comfort and efficiency in every room. Lights can be dimmed and heat can be turned on only in occupied rooms or set to turn off while occupants are away. Solutions such as operable skylights and sunshades create a means for controlling natural ventilation. Control over the atmosphere in your own home will add to your comfort and give you more power to minimize your home's energy use.

**Design for Beauty, Joy, and a Sustainable Life**

Life in a sustainable home is not just about leaving a light footprint on the earth. It is also about living a good life within the walls of that home—a long healthy life of sound quality and brimming with happiness. A thoughtfully designed home will help you enjoy every day you spend there. It will bring friends and family together. It will give you beautiful vistas, inside and out, and improve the quality of the air you breathe. A sustainable home can even, in the midst of chaos everywhere else, offer you moments of peace. Designing a space to help you celebrate life is the final important component of our smart design EcoPrinciple.

## Eco-Materials

We can all practice better environmental stewardship by increasing our awareness of materials in our products and especially our homes. This is the second of our five EcoPrinciples: choose eco-friendly materials whenever possible. It is paramount that materials are sustainably sourced and their shipping and processing leaves a minimal impact on the planet. The following qualities are what we demand from the materials that go into the homes we design; try keeping them in mind when considering materials for anything you buy or build, from your own home to the things you put in it.

**Renewable Materials**—Renewable materials are resources that reproduce quickly and/or are sustainably harvested. Bamboo is a wonderful example of a renewable material. The largest of the grasses, bamboo is the fastest-growing woody plant on earth and can climb ninety feet skyward in one year. Unlike trees, when bamboo is harvested for its wood, the source can easily and quickly be replenished. This is why we like to use bamboo flooring (and the fact that it produces an incredibly beautiful floor too). When choosing your bamboo flooring though, it is important to research various suppliers and choose one that is sensitive to laborers' working conditions and the transport of the product.

**Sustainably Harvested Materials**—Sustainably harvested materials are an important eco-friendly solution too. While bamboo earns the label "sustainably harvested" because it is rapidly renewable, not all woods have it so easy. Fortunately, we have the FSC (Forest Stewardship Council) certification, which requires a forest operation to be socially beneficial and managed in an environmentally appropriate and economically viable manner. An FSC certification also requires a company engaged in manufacturing, processing, or trading timber or other forest products to operate under responsible sourcing policies. We use FSC wood for flooring, cabinetry, and exterior siding—basically anywhere we can.

**"Green" or "Living" Walls**—These are walls that actually give back to the environment. A green or living wall is essentially a vertical garden with plants rooted in fibrous material, anchored to an exterior or even interior wall. These walls are not only beautiful but can also improve air quality. Plant root systems house bacteria that metabolize air impurities such as VOCs (volatile organic compounds).

**Wheatboard and Particleboard**—Wheatboard and particleboard are good choices for cabinet substrates and sheathing. Wheatboard is the greenest option. Made from wheat stalks, which are just the by-product of wheat harvests, wheatboard is formed into panels through heat and pressure. The naturally occurring starch in the stalks acts as the glue to hold the panels together, eliminating the need for artificial glues or formaldehyde. Where wheatboard is unavailable, particleboard, a mixture of wood scraps and glue, is the next best option.

**Recycled Materials**—Recycled materials are made from items that would otherwise be thrown in a landfill but are separated from the trash and remanufactured as a reusable material. Countertops can be made from all sorts of recycled materials such as paper and glass. One countertop we like is made from a fifty-fifty composite of bamboo fiber and recycled wood fiber reclaimed from demolition sites. The two elements are bonded together with a water-based resin. Another countertop option we like is made from concrete with fly ash

This mkSolaire uses tiles created from recycled chardonnay bottles.

or recycled porcelain mixed in. The porcelain used in these countertops would normally end up in a landfill somewhere.

Recycled glass and porcelain can also be created into lovely tiles. Post-consumer glass from windshields, bottles, and windows is crushed, mixed with other ingredients, and then melted into shape, all while using less energy than traditional tile-manufacturing processes. Porcelain from old sinks and toilets can be converted into beautiful tiles as well.

Recycled materials can be used in a variety of places throughout a home, including decking. Composite decking is an environmentally friendly material made from a combination of recycled plastic and sawdust. It never splinters, warps, or needs staining. Even something like carpet, which has traditionally been a very un-green material (and I am not talking about the color), now comes in eco-friendly varieties. The best of these is recyclable carpet tiles made from recycled content and corn-based products. Unlike wall-to-wall carpeting, these tiles reduce waste because a ruined tile can simply be removed and either cleaned in a sink or replaced, while a large carpet must be either deep cleaned, requiring energy and sometimes toxic cleansers, or replaced in full.

**Reduce Waste, Use Less**—We all should take only what we need from the earth's natural resources. It is estimated that more than 90 percent of the raw materials that go into producing durable goods in the United States will immediately go to waste. Another estimate puts the amount of construction waste generated from building an average single-family U.S.

home (about 2,320 square feet) at somewhere between 6,960 and 12,064 pounds. One of the many reasons we use modular technology to create our homes is that we can achieve 50 to 70 percent less waste with it. Building in a factory allows for precision cutting, so each cut is done right the first time.

**Long-Lasting, Low-Maintenance Materials**—Choose materials that require little, if any, upkeep and rarely need replacing. Just as designing for longevity is a part of the smart design principle, choosing materials for their longevity is an important part of the principle of eco-materials. If you choose the right exterior siding, then you eliminate the need to buy paints and varnishes in the future. If you create a roof out of something like weathering steel, you eliminate the need to ever reroof your home. Make smart choices today about the materials that go into your home and reduce the need for maintenance and materials tomorrow.

**Reuse**—Whenever possible, reuse materials. The reuse of old materials is not only more efficient and less wasteful but also can add unique character to a space. A reusable material we are especially fond of is reclaimed wood, which can come from a variety of sources, such as old barns, train tracks and trestles, or any old, demolished wooden structure. The markings of the wood's past life—a weathered look, odd holes, or dings, maybe even a "Billy + Suzy" carving—just add to the personality of it.

**Wood vs. Steel**—Opinions differ as to whether wood or steel is the more sustainable option for framing a home, and no material can offer the perfect solution. While traditional wood framing obviously comes from trees (an eco-negative), it does use 20 percent less energy during manufacturing, emitting significantly less toxins into the air and water during the manufacturing process. Wood framing also thermally outperforms steel by 22 percent and provides carbon sequestration, which lessens global warming. In steel's defense, steel studs are recyclable, stronger, and more resistant to threats like fire, rust, termites, and rot.

On the other hand, engineered lumber is better for the environment than both steel and traditional wood framing. Engineered lumber (also called composite wood) is a general term used to describe a variety of man-made, engineered-wood products. Made from wood scraps, fibers, and sawdust, engineered lumber is bonded together using high pressure, heat, and adhesives to form a composite material. Engineered lumber only uses half the wood of conventional wood framing, and the wood it does use can be obtained from rapidly renewable small-diameter trees, preserving valuable old-growth trees. Engineered lumber is twice as strong as traditional wood framing and more resistant to humidity-induced warping and defects.

It takes more than using recycled products to create an eco-friendly material. We must take into account the entire life cycle of a product or material before deeming it sustainable. The life cycle of a product includes how the original raw material was obtained, the refinements made to the material, its shipping and installation, the material's use, and finally its disposal and recycling capabilities. Very similar eco-friendly products can have widely different environmental impacts. In this country, when we toss something out, the product itself will, on an average, contain only 5 percent of the raw materials that were consumed in the making and delivery of it. We must look at where a material comes from, how it gets to us, and what the future has in store for it in order to understand its true sustainability.

## Energy Efficiency

The following numbers are ones you may have heard before but they certainly bear repeating: within the United States, buildings account for roughly 40 percent of total energy use, 70 percent of total electricity consumption, and 38 percent of total carbon dioxide emissions. As a person who works in the building industry, I am not very happy or proud about these numbers. Luckily, there are a growing number of green-energy options that can be incorporated into a building to increase its efficiency, decrease these percentages, and bring down the totals at the same time. The following innovative energy-efficient technologies are a must for any green home.

**Efficient Envelope**—A tight seal between foundation, roof, walls, doors, and windows is crucial to achieving an energy-efficient building. A building can be a difficult thing to seal, considering its many seams and openings. Adding to this, temperature discrepancies exist between the exterior and interior, resulting in expansion and contraction. Creating a good seal is

possible and can greatly improve energy efficiency. A seemingly small one-eighth-inch gap between your front door and its threshold has the same impact as a two-inch-square hole in your wall. Closing that small gap can save you as much as 15 percent in heating and cooling costs. In fact, one U.S. Department of Energy–sponsored study estimated that an efficient building envelope can save you anywhere from 3 to 36 percent annually on heating and cooling energy costs.

High-quality insulation in a building is like a big warm coat to your body or a door to your freezer. It will keep heat in when outside temperatures are low and heat out when outdoor temperatures are soaring. All our homes are built with an air-barrier, open-cell foam insulation, and all wood-to-wood framing joints are caulked, making them airtight. Proper insulation is a must for an energy-efficient home.

If you think of insulation as your home's winter coat, then you can think of a green roof as your home's winter hat. The plants and soil that make up a green roof provide excellent insulation on top of a building, especially when combined with rigid insulation boards below. In the winter, the green-roof plants trap rising hot air. In the summer months, they not only help trap cool air but also absorb solar heat from above, preventing much of the heat from penetrating into the building.

True energy efficiency is a two-step process: The first step is designing a home and choosing systems that *require* less energy. An efficient building envelope with a tight seal and

Beauty and energy efficiency combine with a green roofing system.

high-quality insulation is the perfect example of this. The second step in true energy efficiency is the choice of *using* less energy by turning off lights, lowering your thermostat, and taking shorter showers, for example.

**Efficient Fixtures**—Installing efficient fixtures (lightbulbs) is an easy way to save energy. Incandescent bulbs, with their short lamp-life and high heat output, are quickly going extinct. Their output and performance is no match for two other types of fixtures on the market now—light-emitting diodes (LEDs) and compact fluorescent lamps (CFLs).

When searching for new bulbs for your home, consider which factors are most important for you. Do you want the most energy-efficient bulb? Do you need a lot of brightness? Do you want to make sure you don't change a lightbulb for a decade? Are you concerned with upfront cost? LEDs and CFLs both offer great energy efficiency but vary in price, lifespan, brightness, and wattage (electricity use to light it).

Light-emitting diodes (LEDs) produce illumination through little bulb-shaped semiconductors and are an excellent alternative to incandescent lights. While the upfront cost of LEDs is still quite high when compared to other bulbs, the LED has a lifespan of 60,000 hours (versus a CFL's 10,000 hours and an incandescent's 1,500 hours). LEDs use the least amount of energy than any other bulb. That said, your LED fixture will be less bright than a traditional or CFL bulb and has a very direct beam of light, which may not be ideal in a table lamp or reading light.

CFLs use florescent instead of incandescent light and, compared to traditional lightbulbs of the same luminous flux, are much more energy efficient. These versatile bulbs can save a whopping 75 percent of the electric costs incurred for each lamp you install. CFL bulbs do not last as long as LEDs but will work up to ten times longer than incandescent bulbs and emit 90 percent less heat, reducing heat gain brought on by interior lighting. CFL bulbs contain some mercury and need to be disposed of properly when they have burned out.

**Efficient Appliances**—Appliances are a part of our everyday lives, and choosing energy-efficient models can go a long way in reducing energy consumption. Luckily, the Energy Star program has made the task of finding energy-efficient appliances a lot easier. Products bearing the Energy Star logo have met strict energy-efficiency guidelines set by the Environmental Protection Agency (EPA) and the U.S.

Department of Energy. An efficient appliance saves money too. An average American home spending about $1,900 annually on energy can save about $80 a year if using more efficient appliances. An Energy Star–certified dishwasher or clothes washer will expend about 50 percent less energy per load than their noncertified counterparts.

**Efficient Heating and Cooling Systems**—Energy-efficient heating and cooling systems are an important part of a green home. If a home needs a combination heating and cooling system, then a high-velocity, mini-duct, forced-air system is the right choice. These systems use narrower ducts than traditional forced-air systems, allowing the air to flow from vents much faster and thus heat or cool a room quicker. A radiant-heating system is another efficient system. A radiant system's heat energy is emitted from a warm floor and warms people and the objects in their rooms rather than heating the air around them. This maintenance-free system achieves the same comfort level but allows the temperature of a home to remain lower than a conventionally heated home.

We have so many options for cooling our homes without turning on our energy-draining air-conditioning systems. For example, most days simply require a ceiling fan—an option that not only uses much less energy but also works quickly and more effectively than air-conditioning. House fans are also great; they

Adjustable louvers on this Breezehouse block the sun's heat.

reside in the ceiling of your top floor, where hot air gravitates naturally. Turning on the house fan will siphon all the hot air out of your home and into the attic while at the same time pulling cool outdoor air into the living spaces.

"Cool roofs," which prevent the sun's heat from penetrating a building, are an energy-efficient cooling alternative to air-conditioning. The material, slope, and even color (usually white) of one of these roofing systems are all designed specifically to reflect the sun's rays and can reduce roof-surface temperature by up to 100 degrees Fahrenheit.

Simply shading a home from the sun can be the most efficient way to cool it. Low-tech sliding wooden sunshades easily slide along a building in the same way that a barn door does. On hot days, sliding wood sunshades can be positioned over large windows or glass doors to block the sun's heat. Louvers and shades are another adjustable sun-shading option. Trellises will also block the sun but because they cannot be adjusted, they must be thoughtfully positioned from the onset. Vegetation, also if strategically placed, can provide very effective and beautiful sun shading.

**Alternative Energy Sources**—Getting our power from renewable resources is one of the best ways to reduce the negative impact of our energy consumption. One of the better-

Photovoltaic panels use energy from the sun and lower your energy bills.

Wind is another plentiful natural resource to harvest for energy. In fact, in the United States alone, we have enough wind blowing around to create triple the amount of energy we use right now. Just as the huge wind turbines you see in sprawling wind farms produce energy (each enough for 400 American homes), small-scale wind turbines can produce energy for your own home. As technology improves, these residential turbines are becoming more accessible and affordable.

An exciting new development in the world of wind power is the ability to use kites for harnessing energy from wind. The concept is still in its infancy but has the potential to generate more electricity from wind than turbines. It is estimated that the kites and associated structures needed to produce energy in this manner would cost only one-fifteenth of what it takes to erect a wind turbine. Kites could also reach higher latitudes, where winds are consistent and stronger.

known alternative-energy sources is solar power. The energy of the sun, even after traveling millions of miles to get here, is powerful and plentiful. Photovoltaic (PV) panels can be installed on a roof or any sunny location within a thousand feet of your home, but not just your home in Hawaii—solar power relies on light, not heat, so even a location that is cold but sunny can still make the most of solar power.

A solar thermal water heater, like PV panels, harnesses the sun's energy but uses it specifically to heat water for your home. This simple device consists of a two-by-four-foot box with a coiled pipe running in and out, and it sits on top of your roof. The box absorbs the heat of the sun, which is then transferred into the water within the pipe. The hot water will then rise up the coiled pipe and out into a standard water-heater tank, where it will be stored. Like PV panels, a solar water heater relies on light and not heat, so it can remain functional during the winter months. The heated water it produces can be converted into heat for radiators, forced-air fans, and radiant-heating systems.

Currently, the cost of installing solar is high but will hopefully begin to decrease as demand and popularity grow. Solar-power systems may have a large initial price tag, but, like any energy-saving investment, it offers payback over time in energy-cost savings. The average time period for recouping your original investment is five to ten years. Some areas offer solar tax rebates, so this time period can vary according to system and region.

Another alternative-energy source for heating water as well as cooling it is geothermal power, which is derived from the natural heat stored beneath the earth's surface. By placing pipes below the frost line and running water through them, you can take advantage of the natural heat of the ground temperature. Geothermal power will warm the water between 50 and 55 degrees Fahrenheit before that water passes through a heat exchanger in your home. The heat exchanger will further raise the temperature of the water in the winter or cool it in the summer.

**Monitoring Systems**—An energy-monitoring system is the best way to learn about your true consumption habits. When we are more aware of our energy consumption, we can change our behavior. Monitoring systems allow you to see, for example, how much lower your energy bills would be if you use your dishwasher at night rather than during the day. Where our energy is going and how much we are using can teach us a lot. This happened to me when I first had my Toyota Prius and began driving it around. For the first time, I could see how my driving behavior directly affected engine performance and my gas mileage. In time, I began to adjust my driving habits to use less gas even though my hybrid already gives me really good gas mileage.

## Water Conservation

Every living thing and every ecosystem on this planet depends on a clean, healthy water supply. This dependency connects us all and also underlines the incredible value water holds. It is easy for Americans to take fresh potable water for granted, but all over the world it is becoming an increasingly scarce resource; 70 percent of the world's water supply is currently considered polluted. Water's vital importance in our lives cannot be stressed enough. This is why water conservation is one of our five EcoPrinciples. The homes we design pay homage to the importance of water by incorporating elements that reduce water intake, reuse water where possible, and minimize storm-water runoff through sound site-water management.

**Reduce Water Intake**—The truism "waste not, want not" applies to water as much as it does to anything else on earth. Per capita, the mean indoor daily water use in today's American homes is slightly over sixty-four gallons, but by taking measures to conserve water, you can reduce usage to fewer than forty-five gallons a day. Because water outlets in a home are usually centralized in bathrooms, kitchens, and perhaps a few outdoor areas, it is easier to zero in on these sources to eliminate waste. For example, bathrooms account for 74 percent of all domestic water usage in the United States; toilets alone comprise 40 percent of all domestic water consumption and become an obvious place to make changes.

Low-flow toilets are a good place to start. These toilets use only 1.6 gallons of freshwater per flush versus the 3.5 the average American toilet sends down the drain. In some states they are actually a requirement. Making the swap will automatically reduce by over 50 percent the amount of water consumed by the one thing using the most water in your home. Low-flow toilets are the least-expensive option for cutting water usage in your home and will save you money on your utility bills. In fact, by using water-efficient fixtures, you can receive cash incentives in some local municipalities that may go so far as to pay for your new low-flow toilet!

Composting toilets are just what the name suggests: toilets that turn waste into compost. They are odor-free and require no plumbing, piping, or sewer lines. Composting toilets are similar to the toilets you find on airplanes. Instead of using

a model of water efficiency, you can retrofit it with an easily installed aerator. While still maintaining water pressure, aerators reduce water flow by two to two-and-a-half gallons per minute (from four) by adding more air to the flow of water.

Localized water heaters do a fantastic job of saving energy and water. The average American home uses a water-heater-and-tank system to get hot water out of the tap, but such a system wastes about 10,000 gallons of water annually per home as people are forced to wait for their water to warm up. The solution to this waste is a tankless on-demand

Low-flow toilets are a good place to start. These toilets use only 1.6 gallons of freshwater per flush versus the 3.5 the average American toilet sends down the drain.

drinkable water, composting toilets use natural chemicals to flush waste, eventually turning it into compost used on your nonfood plants in the garden. They only require an annual clean out (you can hire a professional to do this) and in that year produce about a gallon of compost.

Low-flow showerheads are a necessity for water conservation in the bathroom. Twenty-two percent of North American water use is devoted to showers, which can expend 2.5 to 5 gallons of water for every blissful minute you spend enjoying that nice hot shower. Change out your old showerhead for a water-efficient model and you could save a combined $100 on your water and energy bills. To convert your sink faucet into

water heater that mounts under your sink or on a wall near your bathroom. At the push of a button, a super-efficient gas heater will instantly warm the cold water coming into the bottom of the box before it flows out. The heater will then shut down when you turn off the hot water. On-demand water heaters also save energy because no energy is lost through pipes as hot water travels to an outlet.

Watering a lawn can use about eight gallons of water per minute, so xeriscaping yards and gardens is a smart way to reduce water usage. Xeriscaping simply means landscaping with drought-tolerate plants in a way that will not require a lot of extra water or fertilizer. It is also important to plant species that are indigenous to the specific climate in which you live, especially if that climate is a dry hot one.

Another way to save water in your garden or yard is through the use of drip irrigation. In contrast to the conventional method of sprinkler watering, which just wastes more than half the water you use, drip irrigation works under the soil, where it applies water directly to where it is needed: the roots. The water you save with drip irrigation is enough to pay for the initial cost of the system in as little as one year. Another way to save water outdoors is a weather-tracking system. These clever monitors check weather forecasts and shut off your watering system if rain is expected. As with drip irrigation, this system can pay for itself in water savings within a year.

**Reuse Water**—When freshwater is not needed, then a good substitute is used water. By capturing rainwater runoff from your roof and collecting it all in one place, you can utilize valuable water that might otherwise just wash away. Water-catchment systems do just that: they collect storm water in barrels located either underneath your house or around the exterior. These can then be tapped and the water used to irrigate your landscape when the rainy season ends.

Another thoughtful way to reuse water is through a grey-water system, which can be applied in your home or garden. A grey-

The rainwater catchment system on the mkLotus captures water that might otherwise wash away, and uses it for landscaping.

water system captures and treats old wash water from sinks, dishwashers, and even clothes washers to be reused in place of fresh potable water for flushing a toilet or watering your yard. A whole-house grey-water system includes a collection tank beneath your home where microorganisms will purify the water before it is pumped into a drip irrigation system in your garden.

Alternatively, a smaller-scale system can be used. A bathroom grey-water system captures used sink water, filters and disinfects it, and then sends it to your toilet in place of potable water. If the system runs low on reclaimed water, then it just switches back to the normal toilet valve until the supply is replenished. A grey-water system can save more than 3,000 gallons of fresh water annually—water otherwise destined straight for the sewer. It pays for itself in water savings in about four years and lasts for ten to twelve years total, which equates to six to eight years of just saving money.

**Site-Water Management**—Employing thoughtful site-water-management techniques will minimize storm-water runoff on your land. Storm-water runoff does more than just damage your property; it causes soil erosion and pollution of local water sources. Green roof systems help to reduce runoff because the vegetation and soil on top of your home will absorb much of the rainwater hitting your roof.

Building swales into your landscape will also prove effective in reducing runoff on your land. An unpaved swale, which is just a ledge or depression in the land (also called a vegetative swale or bioswale), helps storm water infiltrate your soil, limiting runoff. In effect, swales capture and treat runoff water by letting it filter naturally through soil and plants, where any pollutants can be safely broken down by microorganisms.

Unlike paving, which contributes to the flow of runoff into the sewer, permeable materials used for walkways and driveways can facilitate the absorption of the rainwater. Many choices for permeable pavement exist, including recycled concrete, reclaimed brick, and salvaged stone. For your driveway, there are a few great options, including pervious concrete (exactly what the name suggests), decomposed granite (granite in pebble form), and grasscrete (a combination concrete-grass system).

## Healthy Environment

When designing a green home, it is imperative to consider the health of the people living inside. Healthy indoor air quality is an essential element of the homes we design and the last of our five EcoPrinciples.

**No Off-Gassing Materials**—A home should not pollute the air inside your home with off-gassing. Many of the materials commonly found in homes release harmful, even carcinogenic gasses in the form of volatile organic compounds (VOCs). An example is latex wall paint, which is full of VOCs

that are known carcinogens and directly related to asthma in children. Considering we spend about 80 to 90 percent of our time indoors, choosing only no- or low-VOC paint for your interiors is an effective way to keep your family healthy.

Formaldehyde, a toxic, allergenic, and carcinogenic indoor pollutant, is another common indoor health threat. Many construction materials on the market use formaldehyde-based resins. Thankfully, many great formaldehyde-free alternatives such as wheat board and FSC-certified wood materials are on the market and can be used for making a home.

**Air Filtration**—Filtered air is cleaner air, so filtration (either natural or electric) should be a part of every home. HEPA (high-efficiency particulate air) filters are a great way to "vacuum" the air you breathe in your home. First developed in the 1940s to prevent the spread of airborne radioactive particles, HEPA filters can remove at least 99.97 percent of the smallest airborne particles in your air. These filters are also used in hospitals to prevent the spread of airborne bacteria and infections. If a HEPA filter is good enough for nuclear labs and hospitals, it is certainly good enough for use in your own home.

**Spray-In Foam Insulation**—Using this high-quality, efficient insulation not only leads to better energy efficiency but also creates a healthier home environment. We use spray-in foam insulation because it offers a barrier that is thirty-seven times more effective than fiberglass batts or boards. The foam, once sprayed, expands to custom fit the framing cavities and to better control moisture, which staves off potential health threats like mold. It also won't off-gas and is the only insulating material certified by the Envirodesic Program for Maximum Indoor Air Quality.

**Hard-Floor Surfaces**—By installing hard-floor surfaces instead of carpeting, you can create a healthier environment in your home. Carpeting, because it is so hard to thoroughly clean, traps health hazards such as mold, pests, and allergens, creating a continuing threat to your family's health. Another factor to consider is that carpeting is generally made from synthetic oil-based materials that release harmful chemicals into the air. Floors made from FSC-certified woods or recycled material tiles are definitely the cleaner, greener choice. If you are the barefoot type who likes the feel of something soft under your feet, then use easily washable carpet tiles over your hard-floor surfaces.

## An Energy Performance Comparison

So how do these EcoPrinciples translate into real savings? A new generation of energy-simulation software offers precise and detailed data for comparing the energy efficiencies of homes. We use EnergyPlus, one of the most advanced software tools in the field of energy comparison. This innovative program can accurately model and compare heating, cooling, lighting, ventilating, and water loads in buildings, allowing us to study different strategies and their effectiveness in local conditions. In addition, EnergyPlus can calculate indirect environmental effects such as atmospheric pollutants, which are linked with a building's energy use. We are able to simulate and model complex systems to ensure our homes are more energy efficient.

We performed an EnergyPlus comparison of two buildings—one a Sunset Breezehouse, using sustainable technologies and energy-efficient systems; the other a typical U.S. home the same size. The Sunset Breezehouse outperformed the traditional home in energy consumption, fuel totals, and carbon emissions. While some of the disparity could be attributed to different energy-efficient systems (such as dual-flush toilets, Energy Star appliances, dual-pane glass, the use of CFLs, and our other tools for building green), a few other differences are worth noting.

The Sunset Breezehouse has a much different plan, or "footprint," than the traditional home in the study. While both homes are around 2,800 square feet, the Sunset Breezehouse only needs to heat or cool 1,996 square feet. With the use of outdoor rooms and smart design, the Sunset Breezehouse feels as large as a traditional home, but energy is not wasted artificially conditioning the extra space. Roofs on traditional homes also tend to be unnecessarily large. This large voluminous space may make sense in France or Maine, but in most climates its sole purpose is simply curb appeal. Heating and cooling this oversized roof quickly translates into unnecessary fuel consumption and large monthly energy bills.

## Green Financial Information

The underlying principle of going green is the idea of using less. Using less means spending less in the long run. For example, when building a home from scratch, building it green will mean using fewer materials during the construction phase. This is why we prefer off-site modular technology. We use fewer materials and create less waste, resulting in lower material costs in the long run.

That said, building and living in a sustainable way can occasionally lead to some sticker shock when you first start out. The upfront costs of green elements for your home like CFLs, PV panels, grey-water systems, and radiant-heating systems may seem prohibitively high in some cases, but it is important to look past the initial price tag and consider the future costs. In most cases, the initial expense of green solutions for the home can be viewed as an investment that pays long-term dividends in the form of money saved on your utility bills. One study performed by Capital E and the University of California found that any green building element will, in its lifetime, pay for itself ten times over. Most green investments offer deferred gratification by paying for themselves in just a few years.

Another thing to remember is that the demand for green products and green building is growing exponentially. This is important financially for two reasons. With more and more people expressing an interest in buying and building green, more products will appear on the market. More products from more manufacturers spur competition, driving prices down. Lower prices mean green solutions are more accessible to more people. We have seen this happen with organic food. When the organic food movement began ten to fifteen years ago, there was only a niche market for organic groceries, and the price was prohibitively high. But over time, the demand for organic food has grown and is now available at lower prices at most stores.

The second important thing to remember is that the demand for green-living solutions is in its naissance. The vast majority of homes in the United States are not green or even energy efficient, though we hope one day they all will be. So right now, as awareness of green building is increasing, studies have shown that the majority of people would be willing to pay more for green-building features in a home (meaning your green home's market value will increase simply because it is green). A sustainably designed and built house may do more than save you money; it may raise the value of your home.

## Green Remodeling

Most of what we have talked about in this chapter and, of course, the rest of this book, pertains to new-home construction. However, there are just as many ways to apply these principles and strategies to existing homes through remodeling and renovation work. Remodeling or renovating your home to make it more sustainable, especially any home built before 1980, is no less important to the health of our environment than constructing a brand-new home sustainably. In fact, if every home in the United States was insulated, it would put an end to our country's dependence on Middle Eastern oil. Put an Energy Star–qualified refrigerator in every U.S. home and we could shut down ten aging power plants.

The key to green remodeling and renovation is to carefully consider any project before diving in. Many people have fallen into the trap of needless wasteful changes in an effort to green their home. You must find the right balance between what should be replaced and what should remain or be reused. Upgraded lighting with new windows or skylights, for example, is a smart investment because it can make your home more energy efficient and your living spaces more beautiful. However, replacing existing wood flooring with eco-friendly renewable wood like bamboo might not be as sustainable as simply refinishing the existing floors. Think of it this way: first do no harm by reducing your waste, then go forth and green your home to your heart's content!

••••

In their book, *Cradle to Cradle*, William McDonough and Michael Braungart paint a vivid picture of two equally energy-efficient office buildings. The first building is based on the concept of unrelenting energy efficiency; the dark-tinted windows do not open, which makes the building both perfectly sealed and immune to the heat of sun. The second building is based on one of their favorite analogies: the ways of the cherry tree. They imagine how an energy-efficient building would look in a world conceived by this naturally efficient yet beautiful tree. The second building would offer outdoor views through large untinted windows as well as individual air and temperature controls for each employee. At night, the cooling system would flush the building with cool night air, and during the day the grass-covered roof would attract songbirds on sunny days and absorb rainwater runoff on rainy ones.

So, do any of the elements listed in the second building sound familiar? In their comparison, McDonough and Braungart admit that both buildings are equally energy efficient, but the second is designed to celebrate "a range of cultural and natural pleasures—sun, light, air, nature, even food—in order to enhance the lives of the people who work there." This is what makes a green home such a beautiful thing; everything about the home is a celebration. When we marry the concept of sustainability to the reality of gorgeous design, the possibilities are endless and tremendously exciting. A green house can be a shrine not just to sustainable living but also to healthful living, connected living, peaceful living, and wholly enjoyable living. We use our five EcoPrinciples to create just that in each of our own home designs. Hopefully, you will be inspired to incorporate some of these ideas in your own home.

A thoughtfully designed home will provide beautiful vistas, inside and out, and improve the quality of the air you breathe.

The mkLotus combines sustainable materials and systems, providing a prepackaged green solution for homeowners.

*It wasn't that we set out to create a company that focuses on prefab. Rather, it turned out to be a means to an end. Prefabrication allows us to prepackage the green solutions. It allows us to combine the different sustainable materials and systems.*

## Green Prefab

*Prefabricated housing,* an all-purpose term used to describe any home that is built partly off-site, is not new. In 1906, the Aladdin Company began selling basic house kits, and between 1908 and 1940, catalog giant Sears, Roebuck and Co. sold more than 100,000 prefab home kits to Americans. Prefab construction processes have been used to create office buildings, schools, and homes for many decades.

After World War II, with many returning veterans in need of inexpensive housing, government-subsidized prefab was embraced as a quick and economical way to meet the increased demand for homes in the United States. As time passed, however, and consumer tastes changed, prefab homes became linked in the public mind with bad design and inferior quality. Today, most people associate prefab with mobile homes that blow away in high winds.

Thanks to a handful of innovative architects and hip shelter magazines, however, prefab is enjoying a revival. In its new incarnation, prefab is catching the eye of design-conscious consumers who appreciate its style and efficiency. Now, "built in a factory" means lower cost and higher-quality building components than many site-built homes. Most importantly, prefab and sustainability are a good match. Green prefab offers a more efficient way of building a home with reduced waste, minimal energy consumption, and smart earth-friendly materials.

## What Is Prefab?

For centuries, architects and craftsmen have traditionally built homes piece by piece, dealing with unreliable weather, inconsistent labor quality, and other obstacles. When materials arrive on-site, they are usually stored outdoors, exposed to the elements. Subcontractor delays and price fluctuations are considered common.

Like the automotive industry did early in the twentieth century, the home-building trade soon realized that pre-built components were a necessity to make construction more efficient. Housing parts in assembly-line production could make building quicker and easier. From roof trusses to prefabricated windows, these premade components could be mass-produced and shipped to the site at much lower costs.

*Prefab* is a catchall term, but fundamentally, it defines any structure that is manufactured in a standard size and can be shipped and assembled elsewhere. Almost all homes today contain some elements of prefabrication, since items like roof trusses, stair treads, doors, and windows are created off-site. Today, many different kinds of prefab homes are readily available on the market: the kit home, the panelized home, the manufactured home, and the modular home, for example. These homes all require land and site work such as grading, foundations, and utilities installation.

**Kit Homes**—These are homes that include all of the basic structural elements and parts required to complete a home. Typically assembled on the site by the homeowner or a contractor, kit homes include log homes, domes, timber-frame houses, and hybrid combinations. Within this category of prefab homes there is great variation in styles, prices, and quality; they can range from a backyard shed to an opulent multimillion-dollar mansion.

The Sears, Roebuck and Co. mail-order homes of the 1900s are an early example of kit homes. Handy homeowners could choose from many designs for around $2,000. The Sears kit included a large instruction manual and 30,000 individual pieces such as lumber, paint, hardware, nails, and appliances. The kit homes of this era even had the option of allowing you to get your mortgage from the company.

Today's kit homes, such as the LV Home by Rocio Romero, typically do not include financing and the kitchen sink. Kit home designers assume that the modern homeowner will hire out for carpentry and construction services. Romero's series includes the standard LV Home, which is a 1,150-square-foot "shell." The two-bedroom, two-bath home kit costs around $35,000 and contains a wall panel system, one interior load wall, steel posts, a roof structure, and metal exteriors.

**Panelized Homes**—A panelized home consists of wall, roof, and floor sections/panels that are made in a factory instead of on a construction site, which allows for better control over waste, cost, and quality of the materials. Structural Insulated Panels (SIPs) are an example of a factory-made panelized system used to replace standard stick framing. SIPs typically are created by sandwiching a thick layer of foam (polystyrene or polyurethane) between two layers of Oriented Strand Board (OSB), plywood, or fiber-cement. SIPs can be precut and customized in a factory, then assembled on-site by fitting splines into precut grooves on the panel edges.

Kieran Timberlake's Chesapeake Bay area Loblolly House, named for the loblolly pine trees indigenous to Maryland, uses a combination of high-tech panels, modules, and preformed structural frames. Its innovative panel-based design draws its inspiration from the automotive, aerospace, and shipbuilding industries. The walls of the home are manufactured with ductwork, wiring, insulation, and plumbing already inside.

**Manufactured Housing**—A term used interchangeably with "mobile homes" or "house trailers," *manufactured houses* are considered portable and temporary structures. The manufactured home is built on a trailer chassis and manufactured off-site using lightweight metal framing. After mobile homes are constructed in a factory, they are transported to a site in a finished state. Little to no on-site labor is required.

Initially, manufactured housing was the category of prefab home sales that thrived after the Second World War. Many returning veterans moved into government-subsidized mobile homes and eventually made these their permanent residences. However, first-generation manufactured housing was not intended to be a lasting accommodation. For safety purposes, the government started regulating manufactured homes and created the U.S. Department of Housing and Urban Development building code (HUD code) in the 1970s. Regulations and codes now distinguish a mobile home from a "HUD-code manufactured home," which is a home built after 1976, but the vernacular has remained the same. In 1994, the government updated the HUD code yet again to include even higher standards for heating, plumbing, electrical systems, structural design, fire safety, and energy efficiency.

**Modular Homes**—As manufacturing technology has advanced, residential construction design pursued more complex prefab components. Eventually, complete home "modules" were able to be built off-site in a climate-controlled environment. These highly engineered modules are stick-built in a factory by skilled craftsmen and transported on trucks, ferries, or trains to a building site, where they are set onto a site-built foundation. Most modules, or "mods," require a short period of finish work. The advantage of modular prefab over kit or panel homes is in the amount of work done off-site. Most of the home is factory built, allowing predictable time and cost

Modules framed in the factory.

Nontoxic foam insulation is applied in the factory.

estimates while maintaining the same, if not higher, quality as stick-built.

Modular homes have all of the characteristics of stick-built homes and must pass the same code requirements. In most cases, modular homes surpass code requirements by incorporating 20 to 30 percent more structure to withstand transport from the factory to the site. Once assembled, a mod cannot be distinguished from its traditionally built counterpart.

General misconceptions and confusion are the biggest reasons why Americans lag behind other countries in their use of off-site building technology. Prefab is already the standard in countries such as Sweden, for example, where more than 70 percent of new homes are factory-built. Many people mistakenly believe that modular housing is the same as manufactured housing. However, modular homes are able to be fully customized, meet higher quality and code requirements, and can be built to any specification or size.

After the devastation of Hurricane Andrew in southern Florida in 1992, a FEMA (Federal Emergency Management Agency) study found that wood-frame modular homes in Dade County, Florida, withstood storm winds more effectively than conventionally built homes. The finding says: "Overall, relatively minimal structural damage was noted in modular housing. . . ." The report also noted that modular homes "provided an inherently rigid system that performed much better than conventional residential framing."

Architects, including Resolution4Architecture, Alchemy

A module ready for transport.

A module arriving on-site.

Architects, and Marmol Radziner, are recognizing the numerous benefits of off-site modular technologies. By decreasing on-site work and increasing factory assembly, architects have greater control over the quality, schedule, and cost of construction. Factory production also reduces construction waste through precise cutting techniques that facilitate the reuse and recycling of excess materials.

## Why We Chose Off-Site Modular Technology

Many incarnations of the prefab home have appeared during the last century, but we are part of a new generation of architects who are modernizing modular. We take the old idea of prefabrication and reshape it to accommodate modern lifestyles and varying climates as well as a commitment to the environment.

We did not set out to create an architectural company that focuses on modular technology. Rather, off-site building turned out to be a preferred means to an end: our commitment to making thoughtful sustainable design that is accessible to all. In our vision for a better way to build and a better way to live, we recognized modular as the way to make it happen.

We knew that clients wanted healthy, simple sustainable homes, but were often too busy to find the solutions. Off-site modular technology allowed us to prepackage the green solutions for clients, combining the different sustainable materials and systems into one neat bundle.

The controlled environment possible in a factory provides higher quality control, more accuracy, and less waste during the building process, resulting in a stronger structure that is better built

The mkSolaire is constructed and installed at the Museum of Science + Industry in Chicago.

Home modules are built off-site in a controlled environment.

The house parts are trucked to the site, where the foundation is already in place.

in a lot less time than the equivalent site-built structures. It takes less fuel and electricity to create a building in six weeks versus seven months, saving our clients time and money.

## How Off-Site Modular Technology Works

Once land and financing have been acquired, we work with our clients to create a floor plan that meets their particular needs and then select options and upgrades to personalize their home. We also work with the clients' contractor to develop the foundation plan, draw up cost estimates, and supervise site work. Customization in the prefab process can happen at many levels, from choosing interior finishes to configuring individualized floor plans and roof types based on client needs. Construction at the site and factory begins after state and local permits have been issued.

In the factory, a modular home is constructed from the inside out, allowing multiple trades to work on the home simultaneously. Inspectors follow and review every step of the home-building process to ensure the highest quality. First, the floors are put together. At the same time, window and door openings are being precisely cut into the wall panels with a horizontal jigsaw. The wall panels are then lifted into place by cranes and attached with bolts and nails to the floor panel. After the walls are bolted into place, spray-in foam insulation is applied to the entire wall cavity. Air is unable to seep through the wall, reducing the probability of moisture and mold issues. In fact, this foam insulation exceeds the American Lung Association's criteria for a healthy home. Once the walls are in place, the electrical wires, plumbing, drywall, and other interior finishes (such as cabinetry and countertops) are installed. The roof, which has been constructed at the same

Once in place, they are bolted down; then button-up work can begin.

time in another part of the factory, is set on top of the walls. Depending on the roof structure and design, the roof can also be installed on-site after the home is set. Finally, exterior siding is applied to the home.

When the mods are complete, they are transported to the site on flatbed trucks. A mod must fit within a single lane on the roadway and be able to avoid power lines and any other overhangs along the way. We always send out a scouting team before contracts are signed to assure the safe delivery of the home. Some sites are too steep or difficult to reach and cannot accommodate a flatbed truck.

While the home is being created in the factory, contractors excavate and pour the foundation on the site. A crane lifts the mods from the truck onto the foundation using heavy-duty

A crane lifts the modules into place.

cables and careful coordination. Once the mods are in place, they are bolted down and the "button up" work can begin. The marriage walls (the area where the mods come together) tie the whole home together but disappear once the home is complete. If the roof was not installed in the factory, it is placed on the home. At this stage, wiring and plumbing

can be connected and any decks, trellises, and landscaping are added.

## A Few Advantages of Off-Site Modular Technology

**Time Savings**—Because the site work and home construction happen simultaneously, the overall construction schedule for modular homes is compressed. The major trades are organized, operating together under supervision. Stick-built construction projects often experience delays as a result of labor-force problems and unpredictable weather. Because of standardized design and construction processes, modular construction is 30 percent quicker to build than conventional on-site construction. Building in a factory nearly eliminates the uncertainties of scheduling that often plague traditional building projects, such as delays or damage due to weather. And with a greatly reduced time line come happy neighbors. The mods come to the site 90 percent complete, so there is significantly less disruption to neighbors.

**Reduced Waste**—Construction waste, which takes up nearly a third of the nation's landfills, is considerably reduced in the modular factory. Precision cutting reduces the amount of materials used, and the remaining scraps, which have never been exposed to the elements, can be stored at the factory for reuse or recycling. We can save 50 to 75 percent in waste compared to on-site building. Theft and vandalism are also diminished since materials are stored in a locked, covered building at all times.

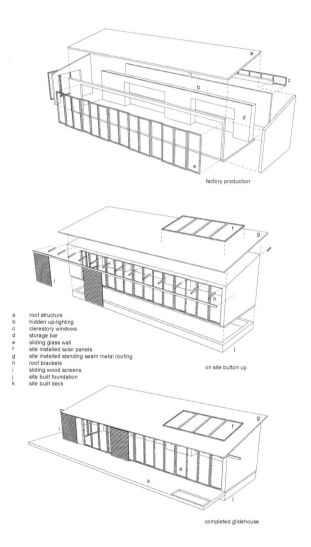

factory production

a   roof structure
b   hidden up-lighting
c   clerestory windows
d   storage bar
e   sliding glass wall
f   site installed solar panels
g   site installed standing seam metal roofing
h   roof brackets
i   sliding wood screens
j   site built foundation
k   site built deck

on site button up

completed glidehouse

Factory production, on-site button up, and completed Glidehouse.

**Quality Control**—A controlled environment means high-quality materials. Materials in our modular factory are stored and assembled indoors, protecting them from warping and mold—a continuous threat when materials are stored and assembled outside. Quality is also increased with our assembly-line construction. Craftsmanship is vital to us. Each home is built by the same specialized construction team, all of whose members are skilled in maximizing time and material efficiency. Our builders precisely assemble materials using level surfaces and horizontal jigs to create a well-crafted home.

**It's Stronger**—Not only do modular homes meet all local, national, and international building codes (UBC/IBC), but they also exceed them. House structure is much sturdier in a modular home than a stick-built one. The mods are built with more structural framing and strapping details to withstand transportation on bumpy roads and the strains of being crane-lifted once they reach the site. Mod-factory workers are also able to use tools unavailable to the conventional builder, such as custom jigs that ensure that all walls, floors, and ceilings are square and plumb.

**Less Gas**—A significant amount of fuel is used to transport labor and materials to sites for conventionally built homes. And while gas is used for transporting the modules, it is offset by the fact that people who work in the prefab factory typically live closer to work than the average contractor or subcontractor who drives to a remote job site. In addition, the shorter time frame for building prefab results in less gas used to get to work. Less fuel and electricity are expended on a home built in twenty-four days (modular) versus seven months (stick-built). Truck transport for materials to the factory could reduce gas usage further. Not only does a prefab home require putting fewer trucks on the road (due to larger loads supplying multiple homes), but also as deliveries become more consistent, the trucking company dispatcher can arrange return loads so the trucks don't come back empty. This level of coordination and fuel savings would be almost impossible to accomplish with a stick-built job site, where deliveries are more unpredictable.

**It's Green**—Off-site modular technology offers many ways to build green and reduce the impact of a home on the environment. Our sustainable approach to building means we make careful decisions at each stage of the planning and construction process. Each home is designed and efficiently built using eco-friendly materials and long-lasting, low-maintenance systems. We use fewer resources and leave far less debris than a typical site-built new house; and we incorporate additional features such as solar panels, water catchment, and grey-water systems, which allow us to achieve even more sustainability.

Modular construction does pose a few challenges. Good prefab is a balancing act; we must balance the level of customization of a home with the efficiencies of mass production in the factory and the limitations (particularly for dimensions) imposed by the shipping process. The appeal of modular construction, however, is that we begin the design process already aware of these challenges, so we can find ways to work around them at the outset.

The original Kaufmann-Cullen Glidehouse.

*We designed our Glidehouse home not for how it looks, but for how it functions. We feel we have an intimate connection to the landscape by living here. We don't need lights on during the day, and we never use air-conditioning. Our home has clean spaces and a real feeling of calm.*

## Glidehouse

Light, simplicity, and sustainability—these are the inspiration for the Glidehouse. In 2001, when my husband and I were looking for an affordable home to buy in the San Francisco Bay region, we were frustrated by the lack of options. From this challenge, however, came our determination to create an alternative, and the Glidehouse was born.

Our first imaginative venture into green modular housing is a light-filled, energy-efficient home created from sustainable pre-fabricated materials. The name Glidehouse comes from the unique sliding glass and wooden doors placed throughout the home; the doors open to the outside and also conceal storage areas. Light streams through well-placed windows, and outdoor spaces fit artfully around the house's modular form.

Like the barns of my childhood home in Iowa, the Glidehouse is designed for function and climate. As Dan Gregory of *Sunset* magazine noted, "It is hard to find a badly designed barn," and it is easy to see why barns, with their uncomplicated, pleasing proportions, are so inspiring. The barn design allows light in through the main doors and utilizes small ventilation openings to allow air circulation. While designing the Glidehouse, I took note of the barn's natural lines, flexible spaces, rich patina of colors, and use of ventilation and natural light, and incorporated these concepts into the home.

The Glidehouse is modular, but it is also flexible. Recognizing that different people have different needs for their homes, we created designs ranging from a small cottage to a four-bedroom model. One of the keys to creating the ideal home is to select the design that best suits the clients' personalities. Glidehouse owners can choose one or two stories, with or without views or a courtyard, for example, and we offer a range of healthy sustainable materials and finishes that allow Glidehouse owners to personalize their homes.

But flexibility and sustainability are only part of the spirit of this home. The design of the Glidehouse is intended not only to please the eye but also the soul. How it looks matters less than how it makes you feel when you are inside.

## The Kaufmann-Cullen Glidehouse

The first Glidehouse was our own residence. Since we wanted an affordable home, we knew that much of the challenge in designing the Glidehouse would be making it "feel" big even though the square footage was modest. We created models to study light and window placement. Recognizing that smart design choices can drastically reduce a homeowner's reliance on energy-demanding air-conditioning systems, we also studied prevailing breeze patterns. Our own negative experience with unhealthy indoor air in a rental home convinced us that the design of the Glidehouse should prevent unhealthy mold and moisture accumulation. The home's foam-cell insulation and green materials ensure a healthy, clean indoor environment.

The interior of the Glidehouse embraces form, function, and aesthetics. Light-colored, rapidly renewable bamboo flooring and an elegant open floor plan make the home appear spacious. A stepped kitchen island screens clutter without closing off the space to other rooms. One of the more notable features of the home is an FSC-certified wooden storage bar that stretches along an entire wall of the living room space. The wooden bar, with its sliding doors, not only offers considerable storage options but also is easily customized. It can be designed to accommodate collections of books, artwork, or any number of other objects. This allows the living space to remain open and uncluttered, adding to the spacious feeling of the Glidehouse.

The Glidehouse living area.

Sliding doors and wood screens extend the home's usable space.

Like a barn, the Glidehouse is made with long-lasting, low-maintenance materials.

**Upper:** A kitchen made with FSC-certified cabinetry, efficient appliances, and clerestory windows for natural ventilation. **Lower:** Glass doors placed throughout the home maximize cross ventilation and natural lighting.

The wooden bar with sliding doors offers considerable storage options and is easily customized.

We are committed to sustainable living, so the Glidehouse was designed to have as little impact as possible on the environment. The dual-pane glass windows and doors placed throughout the home maximize cross ventilation and natural lighting while minimizing the need for artificial lighting and climate control. The main living space features a long wall made of sliding glass that, when open, allows natural light and air to flow through the home, reducing dependence on central air-conditioning. Ample kitchen windows bathe surfaces with natural light, and strategically placed skylights and windows offer privacy and light in bathrooms. Bedrooms in the Glidehouse feature clerestory windows and sliding glass doors to further promote natural lighting and ventilation, as do exterior gliding wood sunshades.

The sloped roof of the Glidehouse encourages hot air to move upwards and quickly out of the house, and it is designed to accommodate the placement of solar panels. LED and fluorescent lighting as well as Energy Star appliances all promote energy sustainability. The sliding doors and wood screens further extend the home's usable space by opening onto generous decks and a stunning view.

The merging of sustainability and good looks is best observed in the exterior of the Glidehouse. Here, long-lasting, low-maintenance materials such as cor-ten steel provide warmth and allow the home to nestle unobtrusively into its hillside lot. Unlike the cold harsh image that steel conjures in most people's minds, cor-ten steel is almost velvet-like in its appearance and texture, a tactile material reminiscent of the beautiful rusted steel structures of my childhood home in Iowa.

Borne out of our own personal struggle to find a warm, well-designed home, this first Glidehouse has now become a model for sustainable living. I hope the integrity and flexibility of its design ensures that it will continue to do so.

## The Glidehouse at Sunset Headquarters

Word of our Glidehouse spread quickly, and Dan Gregory at *Sunset* magazine, based in Menlo Park, California, invited MKD to build a Glidehouse on Sunset's property for the annual Sunset Celebration Weekend in 2004. After meetings with Dan, Peter Whiteley, and Beth Whiteley at Sunset, we devised a plan for a Glidehouse home to function as an educational green building.

The Glidehouse at Sunset Headquarters.

A prefab modular company based in Agassiz, British Columbia, built the first 1,344-square-foot, two-bedroom, two-module Glidehouse in its factory in only nineteen days. After a 1,300-mile journey, the Glidehouse was delivered to Menlo Park and outfitted with a meditation courtyard, outdoor kitchen, fire pit, and "Ultimate Deck" designed by Peter Whiteley, garden editor of *Sunset* magazine.

Building the Glidehouse home was an exercise in teamwork, and a collaborative spirit prevailed. Because this was our first home built in a factory, the project posed many new challenges and had to be completed on a tight schedule. Despite the obstacles, the team successfully positioned the house in a few hours and completed the "button up" process in only seven days. Landscaping, decking, and interiors were installed a few days later, and the first green prefab Glidehouse was ready for public viewing.

The light-filled kitchen and dining area with bamboo flooring.

The Glidehouse was outfitted with a meditation courtyard, outdoor kitchen, fire pit, and "Ultimate Deck."

Built-ins and ample storage space in each room of the Glidehouse.

The master suite.

Doors open to lovely outdoor rooms.

Once inside, visitors walked through the light-filled kitchen, living, and dining areas, all contained within one module. Sustainable materials such as lightweight composite concrete countertops, FSC-certified birch cabinetry, and bamboo floors were used to showcase environmentally friendly materials and products.

The master suite, guest room, and guest bath occupied the second module. Built-ins with ample storage space, unique sliding wood screens, and mechanical systems to support healthy air not only proved popular with Glidehouse visitors but also became sources of inspiration for our future homes.

In addition to being our first factory-built green home, the Glidehouse achieved something even more significant. This new home demonstrated to the community that green design

wasn't merely a trend, nor was it something that only the elite could afford. The Glidehouse represented a new philosophy of sustainable design—one that made green living and beautiful spaces an attainable choice for all homeowners.

## The Reid Glidehouse

Andrew Reid, a Seattle-area mortgage lender, his wife, Kindra, and their son wanted a weekend haven away from their frenzied lives in the city. The family had been searching for a vacation home in the Lake Chelan area of the state, about three hours east of Seattle, when Reid came across some information about the Glidehouse. "Both the incredible aesthetics of the Glidehouse and its sustainable construction were huge draws for us," explains Reid.

Lake Chelan and the Lake Chelan Valley are located in central Washington State, nestled in the North Cascades National

The sliding wood sunscreens offer shade while still letting in the breeze.

The Reid Glidehouse in Lake Chelan, Washington.

Park. Lake Chelan, with its 50.5 miles of pristine cobalt water, provides a dramatic backdrop for clean sustainable architecture. The Reids' site, rugged and remote, boasts remarkable views of the glacier-fed lake, mountains, and vineyards.

In 2004, six months after closing on the lot, the Reids moved into their 1,600-square-foot, three-bedroom, 2.5-bath Glidehouse. We customized the vacation home by adding a third bedroom for guests and reconfiguring the design to fit the new locale and extreme weather. Outdoor patios and a swimming pool were also added to enlarge the Reids' usable space and to further enhance their outdoor lifestyle.

One of the Reid home's most majestic assets is the sweeping view. To make the most of these views, we designed the home to face south, toward the lake, a decision that also allowed us to utilize the prevailing breezes and to get the most sun for the roof-mounted solar panels. With an exterior of galvanized metal siding, the home blends elegantly into the site.

"What's really magic about the house is its beauty," says Kindra Reid, a Seattle native. "Outside, it's somewhat industrial

Sliding panel doors reveal a built-in buffet.

Sustainable countertops and cabinetry with energy-saving fixtures are in every bath.

Beautiful views from the Glidehouse dining room.

The perfect family home: functional, sustainable, beautiful, and affordable.

looking, but inside it's a celebration of nature. There are bamboo floors and wooden cabinets. There's rugged stone tile in the bathroom, and when you stand in the shower, the floor feels like the real ground. I used to associate contemporary with cold impersonal spaces, but this house has completely changed that. It's like living in a Japanese garden."

## The McElroy-Walker Glidehouse

When Ami McElroy, her partner, Crista Walker, and their young daughter outgrew their Seattle bungalow, they discussed building their own house outside the city. Reasonably priced options were difficult to find, and they quickly grew discouraged at the cost of custom-built homes. While reading the *Wall Street Journal* one weekend, Crista saw an article on modern prefab design and environmental sensitivity. It was

Clean lines and thoughtful storage in the kitchen area.

To maintain the beautiful view, stainless steel cable railings and guardrails were used throughout the home.

Inviting spaces and beautiful views.

The McElroy-Walker Glidehouse being transported and set on the island of Vashon, near Seattle.

precisely what they were looking for. "We subscribe to living light on the land, cleanly and simply," says Crista, "and everything just clicked."

Ami and Crista researched sustainable options, met with us, and purchased a 1,520-square-foot, three-bedroom, two-module Glidehouse for their lot on Vashon, a small rural island west of Seattle. We personalized the standard Glidehouse design to accommodate the couple's needs as well as the narrow hillside lot. The close relationship of the house and the site ultimately makes the living experience more enjoyable. It also made design and construction more challenging.

The customized floor plan needed to adhere to the narrow width of the lot while still maximizing the lovely views of Puget Sound and Mount Rainier. We minimized the challenges and expense of grading the site by constructing a lower level the family now uses as a light-filled playroom. Crista calls it her dream house, praising its clean lines, efficient use of space, and thoughtful design elements "down to the drawer pulls."

We chose low-maintenance, long-lasting Galvalume and Hardipanel cement board for the exterior. Large sliding glass doors open onto a large composite deck made from recycled grocery bags and reclaimed wood waste. Ami and Crista enthusiastically opted for standard finishes rather than upgrades in order to stay within their budget and to eliminate the need to "make a thousand decisions," as Ami says.

The inviting spaces and beautiful views of the McElroy-Walker Glidehouse all combine to create the perfect family home: functional, sustainable, beautiful, and affordable.

## The Remick Glidehouse

Kim and Conie Remick, both retired telecom workers, wanted to downsize from the large tract home they owned in Rohnert Park, California, to a smaller custom-built home on the forty-one-acre hillside parcel of land they had purchased in the city of Ukiah. Protected by coastal mountain ranges, Ukiah is a gem of a small town nestled in the rugged California landscape.

The Remicks also wanted to lower their carbon footprint and make their new home eco-friendly. They eagerly explored using materials such as straw bale and rammed earth but discovered that the cost of building with these was too high. Their research into sustainable home building brought them

A detached office is a short walk away from the main home.

The energy-efficient kitchen features FSC-certified cabinetry and sustainable countertops.

The Remick Glidehouse.

Sliding wood sunscreens open to beautiful outdoor spaces.

to us, and soon they were on their way to building an efficient, environmentally responsible home.

Our plan for the Remick Glidehouse consisted of three modules. Two of the modules were linked and a third module functioned as a detached office. The home includes glass on three sides to maximize the impressive 270-degree views of the Bonterra Vineyards below. The rusting cor-ten steel exterior of the home fits the wine country vernacular flawlessly—an ideal combination of local context and modern clean lines.

The Remicks enjoy spending time outdoors, so open-air rooms were of particular importance to them. California landscape designer Nick Thayer created a series of beautiful outdoor spaces.

Owner Conie Remick couldn't be happier: "This home provides us nothing more than is needed. It's smaller, more self-sufficient. The green-building technologies just blew us away."

"We have always been fans of green building and looked at many different solutions, but none of them worked. We wanted to do something different, and this Glidehouse is it."

Solar panels generate ample power for the home.

The Remick's Glidehouse living room.

The Haney-Yu Sunset Breezehouse.

*Sunset magazine is this historical entity that offers legitimacy to the virtues of prefabricated housing. I want to get the message across that green design can be affordable and is an alternative to what developers are offering.*

## Sunset Breezehouse

Designed in partnership with *Sunset* magazine, the Sunset Breezehouse is a great example of indoor-outdoor living. The design of the home draws on inspirations as diverse as Italian villas and "dogtrot houses" of the 1800s, with rooms centered on courtyards and private gardens that seamlessly integrate indoor spaces with the outside.

Every room in the home has a corresponding outdoor space—bedrooms open up to courtyards, a private deck complements the master bedroom. Like the flexible light-filled design of the original Glidehouse, our Sunset Breezehouse embraces and respects the environment and represents a continuation of our EcoPrinciples (see pages 35 to 59) of doing more with less and combining beauty and sustainability.

# The Sunset Breezehouse Concept

The idea for the Sunset Breezehouse emerged when *Sunset* magazine editors Dan Gregory and Peter O. Whiteley began talking with me about sustainable homes of the past. Although green design has become popular in our era of abundant technologies, we looked back to the design strategies of a century ago, before artificial lighting and mechanical systems were commonplace in homes, to learn about ways to integrate sustainability and comfort in the Sunset Breezehouse.

The dogtrot house, for example, was a vernacular building form used throughout the 1800s and early 1900s. Typically found in rural, hot, humid areas of the southeast, dogtrot homes are bisected by a center hall or space, creating almost two homes in one. The sheltered center between the two living spaces provides a shaded, well-ventilated area for gathering.

We designed the living and dining areas (known as the breezespace) in the home so that they function similarly to the dogtrot center space but with a modernized twist. The front and back walls of the breezespace, constructed entirely of glass, slide or fold apart to open the living area to the outside. Breezes and exposure to the outdoors can be controlled by adjusting the energy-efficient, dual-pane glass walls.

The high-breezespace ceiling is positioned under a distinctive butterfly-shaped roof designed to conceal the glare from its solar panels. Sculpted light washes over the ceilings and extends down to the center of the living space. During the day, the stone floors throughout the breezespace absorb the sun's rays and then release warmth at night, providing a form of passive solar heating.

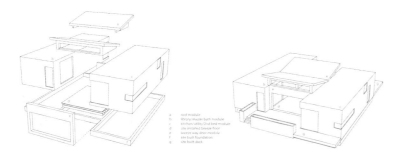

a roof module
b library/master bath module
c kitchen/utility/2nd bed module
d site installed breeze floor
e breeze way door module
f site built foundation
g site built deck

A breezespace opens to the outdoors.

The Sunset Breezehouse also draws on the historical influence of Italian courtyard buildings. Characterized by a U-shaped arcade, the courtyard plan provides access to outdoor space while still offering privacy.

We reimagined the classic U-shaped design of the Italian courtyard building as an H-shaped structure with two modular wings, creating two courtyards instead of one. The airy breezespace opens between one or both courtyards, making the main living-dining space feel much larger and connected to the landscape. Additionally, the same stone flooring extends from the interior breezespace into the exterior courtyard, creating the illusion of one airy luminous space.

The Sunset Breezehouse's H-shaped floor plan works well not only for outdoor spaces and environmental systems but also for modular technology as well. The two-side modules encompass the kitchen, bathroom, laundry, mechanical room, and bedrooms, and meet the height restriction for modular transporting. The soaring breezespace is created by installing roof modules on top of the two-side living modules—a simple method for creating an impressive space.

In keeping with our design philosophy, no space is wasted in the home. Hallways are wide to encourage air circulation as well as to accommodate a built-in desk and information center. The master bedroom closet walls double as a headboard for the bed, providing built-in storage. Even the design of the garage links flexibility with forward thinking: glass garage doors on either side of the garage unit open, allowing the garage space to be used as a potential studio, home office, or play space instead of simply a storage area for a family's vehicle. As in the rest of the home, the garage space makes abundant use of natural light and fresh air.

Doors open to outdoor eating and living areas.

The challenge of building on narrow lots prompted the design of the SideBreeze.

The challenge of building a Sunset Breezehouse on smaller narrow lots prompted us to design the two-story SideBreeze. Unlike the standard Sunset Breezehouse, in the SideBreeze, the two living modules are stacked and the breezespace is moved to the side of the home. Although not as wide as the Sunset Breezehouse, the SideBreeze still offers courtyards off the living areas and an additional storage bar flanking one end of the breezespace.

The Sunset Breezehouse embodies our careful commitment to healthy living and sustainable construction just like the Glidehouse did. Low-VOC paints; formaldehyde-free, FSC-certified cabinetry; recycled reclaimed materials; on-demand water heaters; water-saving plumbing fixtures; and energy-efficient mechanical systems are just a few of the environmentally responsible elements inside the home.

After the success of the Glidehouse at Sunset's Celebration Weekend in 2004, Sunset magazine asked us to join them in designing a second green modular home. Dan Gregory, Sunset's home editor, was an essential member of the team. "Our objective in developing the Sunset Breezehouse was to provide a contemporary, outdoor-oriented, architect-designed modular home with wide market appeal. It's like a reinvented sustainably built Gen-X version of the Eichler atrium production house of the 1960s."

The modules for the Sunset Breezehouse were constructed in two months in a factory near Vancouver, British Columbia, before being transported to the Sunset campus in Menlo

The master bedroom closet wall doubles as a headboard for the bed, providing built-in storage.

The Sunset Breezehouse at *Sunset* magazine headquarters.

Park, California. With the help of many volunteers, site work was completed in ten days; *Sunset* magazine staff then furnished and styled the home. Peter O. Whiteley, *Sunset*'s senior home editor, designed and built outdoor rooms surrounded by attractive native grasses. A beautiful open-air kitchen, lounge area, and spa maximize the home's functional living space. On the eve of the Breezehouse opening, Yvonne Stender, *Sunset*'s style editor, carefully chose no-VOC paint colors for a few key locations and painted well into the night.

The 2005 Sunset Breezehouse drew an impressive crowd. Over the course of two days, 24,000 visitors streamed through the two-bedroom, 1,750-square-foot model of sustainable design. "The Sunset Breezehouse home rides the new wave of interest in architect-designed modular housing solutions," says Dan Gregory. "It provides the highest standard of design for a wide audience while streamlining the building process."

Michelle Kaufmann in the factory with the Sunset Breezehouse.

Indoor-outdoor living.

The airy breezespace opens between one or both courtyards.

The Sunset Breezehouse library with FSC-certified woodwork and no-VOC paints.

Personal touches make this home a unique haven.

# The Komoto Sunset Breezehouse

The Komoto family's three-bedroom, three-module Sunset Breezehouse, located in the East Bay area of California, rests near mountain views and beautiful mature trees. The lot is part of a conventional neighborhood, with homes spaced fairly close together. The challenge in designing the home was to make the most of the view and to create pleasant indoor-outdoor spaces without sacrificing privacy.

We created a quiet secluded space by designing a bamboo wall between the driveway and courtyard. This solution not only provided protective screening for living spaces but also created a defined entry to the home. Clerestory windows, a feature in every Sunset Breezehouse, brought in natural light and fresh air. The windows also maximize the home's views without sacrificing privacy. Clever landscaping and strategically placed walls along the back of the lot also work to screen views and offset traffic noise behind the site.

Thanks to Fu-Tung Cheng, a Berkeley-based designer, the Komoto Sunset Breezehouse includes a number of unique traits. Cheng collaborated with the Komotos to create custom concrete elements such as planters, islands, and a pool, all using natural and found elements. Cheng, known for his inventive understated use of concrete, tied the house beautifully to its site. Using well-placed engawa (Japanese verandas) and a bubbling reflecting pool, Cheng distinguished the intimate outdoor area off the master bedroom from the more public courtyard space.

The Komoto Breezehouse rests in a conventional neighborhood with views and mature trees.

Copper rain chains and other Japanese accents create a Zen calm throughout the courtyard spaces.

Glass accordion doors can be modulated to let in breezes.

The breezespace opens to a beautiful outdoor room, expanding the family's usable space.

Clean lines and the Komotos' personal touches make this home a unique haven. Their residence may sit within a bustling traditional neighborhood, but it retains a sense of peaceful seclusion.

## The Rockne-Andreas Sunset Breezehouse

Ellen Rockne, an accomplished singer and artist, and Brian Andreas, a talented writer and artist, owned a lush garden lot in a beautiful neighborhood near downtown Santa Barbara. Cofounders of an imaginative performance and storytelling company, the couple approached us with a commitment to creating a cutting-edge "fully green" home.

Ellen and Brian made a movie showing their existing lot, which contained an old studio structure and neighboring tower. It was a great way for us to understand the site, and we knew immediately we could play off that tower. Due to existing conditions, site limitations, and the needs of the clients, we designed a custom three-bedroom-plus-studio Sunset Breezehouse. One side of the home became a two-story structure, and the one-story side took the neighboring tower as its background, blending and connecting the new with the old.

We were delighted to discover the owners planned to "deconstruct" the existing home/studio. Deconstruction, an alternative to demolition, involves taking a structure apart by hand and salvaging as many of the pieces as possible, which creates less waste in landfills. Just before the deconstruction, the ever-creative couple gathered friends and neighbors for a "graffiti party," where everyone lavishly painted the interior and exterior of the soon-to-be-deconstructed home.

While Ellen and Brian loved modern lines and warm materials, they are also thoughtful neighbors who wanted their home to fit comfortably into the existing community. To achieve this, we created a modern spin on the local storybook Spanish-California style. The choice of exterior materials was the key to this. Cor-ten rusted steel was chosen for the outside of the home; its dark-red-and-brown palette mimics the clay-tile roofs of many of the neighboring homes. We also added accent walls made of sustainably harvested Ipe wood to create a warm natural-looking exterior.

Ellen Rockne actively collaborated with us, researching sustainable materials and systems for her new home. Since sun shading is critical in Santa Barbara, we crafted a system of operable trellis louvers over the courtyard. The louvers can be opened in the morning or throughout winter, when extra light and warmth are needed, but they can be closed in late afternoon and during the summer, when the sun becomes too intense. Another innovative louver system was also installed on a sliding track for the three bedrooms on the second floor. These sleek louvers act as a screen, allowing ventilation into the bedrooms while shielding them from the intense light.

Large boulders excavated during the site work were collected and used as design elements in the central garden. The courtyard between the breezespace and studio

*continued, page 113*

The Rockne-Andreas Sunset Breezehouse: a modern spin on the local Spanish-California style.

Left: The Rockne-Andreas' often-used detached artist studio.

The fully green home was created with sustainable and recycled materials.

Cor-ten rusted steel was chosen for the exterior; its dark-red-and-brown palette mimics the clay-tile roofs of many of the neighboring homes.

The louvers act as a screen, allowing ventilation into the bedrooms while shielding them from the intense light.

provided the ideal location for Ellen's singing performances. The landscape is designed to accommodate an audience while Ellen uses the breezespace as an ad hoc stage.

Unlike many clients who desire screening from neighbors and roads, Ellen and Brian had a different outlook. The couple wanted a feeling of connection to their neighborhood's street life. "We want to bring back the front porch," says Ellen. "We plan to sit on the front deck and talk to people as they walk by."

## The Dry Creek Valley Sunset Breezehouse

Blessed with some of the most beautiful scenery in the world, Dry Creek Valley in Sonoma County encourages a private and simple lifestyle. The owners of an idyllic property in wine country approached us to create a home that connected to the lush hillsides and picture-perfect vineyard surrounding it.

Collaborating with landscape architects Deakin and Vanozzi, we positioned the breezespace to take full advantage of vineyard views. The two-bedroom Sunset Breezehouse's form and color palette complement the neighboring barn, and a trellis made of woven wood was added to filter sunlight over the outdoor rooms and to blend with Sonoma's architectural heritage.

Like most wine-country residents, the clients enjoy alfresco dining and spending time outdoors among the vineyards. We paid close attention to the home's open-air rooms—framing the landscape, providing shade, and harnessing breezes to

A trellis made of woven wood filters sunlight over the outdoor rooms and blends with Sonoma's architectural heritage.

The home was customized to reflect the clients' distinctive passions and tastes.

The home is connected to the lush hillsides and picture-perfect vineyard surrounding it.

Like most wine-country residents, the clients enjoy alfresco dining with vineyard views.

create a peaceful home intricately linked to the land. The interiors were designed by Steven Miller, who customized the home to reflect the clients' distinctive passions and tastes.

## The Haney-Yu Sunset Breezehouse

San Geronimo, California, the site of the Haney-Yu home, is a small town located only thirty-five miles from the Golden Gate Bridge in Marin County. Arriving at the residence is a little like the opening scene in a movie. The project site rests on a flat bluff surrounded by three and half acres of forest and rolling hills with incredible views.

Engaging the beautiful scenery throughout the house was one of our main goals. We designed Glen Haney and Wing

Yu's 1,622-square-foot, two-story Sunset Breezehouse to include three bedrooms, extensive shelving for their book collection, and a basement wine cellar.

The design of the home's outdoor rooms and their relationship to the land and views was of particular importance. And the colors and materials of the home appear to be directly taken from the natural landscape. Warm cedar siding with grey cement-board accents were used on the exterior of the home, nestling it beautifully into the site. Once inside, the warm natural palette is echoed in slate flooring, golden bamboo flooring, and a custom modern fireplace in the breezespace.

Engaging the beautiful scenery throughout the house was one of our main goals.

The warm materials and sweeping views make the breezespace the perfect space for entertaining.

The Haney-Yu kitchen.

The bathroom features recycled mosaic tiles.

The high breezespace ceiling in this Sunset Breezehouse is positioned under a distinctive butterfly-shaped roof. Sculpted natural light washes over the ceiling and extends down to the center of the living space.

The breezespace of the Haney-Yu home.

The outdoor rooms, decks, and roof gardens of
the mkSolaire provide space and breathing room.

*The roofs and windows address the lighting and ventilation challenges of the standard row house by sculpting natural light and fresh air into the center of the home.*

## mkSolaire

The mkSolaire is a clean and stylish home intended for healthy, green living in an urban context. Modeled after single-family row houses but incorporating the spaciousness of a loft, the mkSolaire uses strategically designed roofs and windows to invite light and air into the home.

Like all of our designs, this home is completely solar and uses nontoxic, recycled, and renewable materials. Designed for smaller city lots, the home uses outdoor decks and roof gardens to provide something all too rare in an urban environment: a healthy sense of space and breathing room in the middle of the city.

Since the 1980s, with the rise of the New Urbanism movement, city living has again become an appealing alternative for many people. Row houses, popular in many large cities, are not only efficient in size and resource consumption but also able

A section-cut diagram of an mkSolaire home.

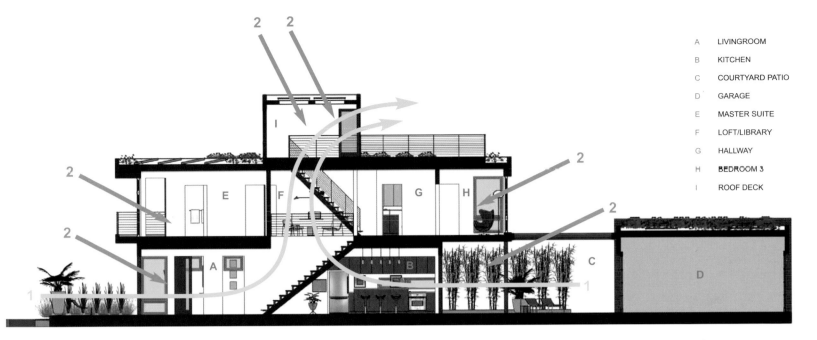

| A | LIVINGROOM |
| B | KITCHEN |
| C | COURTYARD PATIO |
| D | GARAGE |
| E | MASTER SUITE |
| F | LOFT/LIBRARY |
| G | HALLWAY |
| H | BEDROOM 3 |
| I | ROOF DECK |

1   CLERESTORY WINDOWS PROVIDE CROSS VENTILATION THROUGHOUT
    HOUSE, CREATING A 'CHIMNEY EFFECT'

2   BALANCED DAYLIGHTING / INDIRECT LIGHTING WASHES SURFACES
    WITH LIGHT

to adapt with varying housing needs. Vertically organized homes create a smaller footprint and conserve land, supporting the principles of sustainability.

The mkSolaire is our interpretation of the row house paradigm. It fits seamlessly into diverse, existing urban neighborhoods yet still fosters a sense of peace amid the hectic pace of the city. The home incorporates updated green technologies but retains the historic spirit of an original row house.

Despite its small footprint, the mkSolaire's double-height interiors, large windows, and open floor plan create a loftlike space that feels big. Dramatic vaulted ceilings, large skylights,

and an abundance of operable windows allow a generous amount of light and ventilation into the center of the home.

The home is urban and contemporary but not cold or aggressively modern. A simple neutral palette of colors and warm natural finishes create a sense of casual luxury and subdued sophistication. The home is organized in a way that is both functional and modern: the main living area on the first level is spacious and flexible, and serves as the dining and lounging area. The layout is open yet cozy at the same time. Walls of glass bring light and breezes inside, while a fireplace and built-in storage units echo traditional row house elements. The kitchen, which is situated just off the main living space, is cleverly positioned so that it is not completely visible. And in a nod to the more traditional row house, the mkSolaire includes a butler's pantry for easily accessible storage between the kitchen and dining spaces.

Glass garage doors and warm wood siding provide a beautiful backdrop for outdoor eating.

Looking up towards the mkSolaire's light-filled staircase.

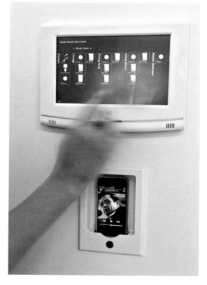

The mkSolaire included energy metering and smart home automation systems.

The mkSolaire's top level provides outdoor deck space and a nice view of the home's green, living roof.

As with all of our designs, the home succeeds in blurring the boundary between the indoors and the outside. Large folding glass doors flank the entire first-floor living area, creating a sheer, subtle separation between the first floor and the outdoor garden and patios. Sheltered porticos and green roof terraces offer shade and refuge from the city beyond and also encourage homeowners to extend their living space into the outdoors.

The ceiling above the main living area stretches from twelve to eighteen feet high and opens up to the airy loft/library on the second level. The second-floor balcony reinforces the cantilever of the upper volume/floor and also provides an overlook to street life below. A roof-access level is available for additional outdoor decking or garden space. The fully functional windows on the roof level create a chimney effect that naturally ventilates and cools the home.

Flexibility is another key element of the design of the mkSolaire. The home is easily adaptable for sloped lots, and additional windows and doors can be added to the sides of the home to accommodate a more suburban setting. Garages and carports are changeable to allow for various configurations and uses. In addition, the home can stand alone or be grouped together to form a duplex or multifamily community.

Depending on the conditions of the site, we offer and encourage a variety of renewable-energy alternatives for

The MSI mkSolaire being constructed in the factory.

As the mods were being constructed, the foundation was being set at the museum.

the mkSolaire, including green roofs, daylighting, geothermal systems, wind generator systems, and other energy hybrids.

## The Museum of Science + Industry mkSolaire

The Museum of Science + Industry is one of the oldest and most beloved science museums in the United States. Located in the city of Chicago, the museum is one of the most popular tourist destinations in the city, attracting about two million visitors per year.

The MSI chose the mkSolaire for their "Smart Home: Green + Wired" two-year-long exhibit. Unveiled in May of 2008, the display is a wonderful resource for people interested in sustainable design. The home showcases sustainable modular construction and green living, and surpassed the Chicago Green Homes

three-star rating system by 50 percent. The MSI mkSolaire, a series of six modules, was built in a factory and then shipped to Beaver Park on the southeastern side of the museum.

The display can educate the public about sustainable design, particularly its ability to be uncomplicated, attractive, and affordable. The interactive Smart Home includes examples of sustainable living, ecological materials, renewable energy systems, smart design, and eco-friendly furnishings. We hope to show that living green doesn't mean you can't live well; it means embracing a healthier, more efficient lifestyle, with all the same style and comfort of a traditional home. "Truth Windows" give visitors a glimpse into one of our modular walls to show energy-efficient foam insulation, the high-velocity mini-duct system, radiant flooring, and engineered lumber. The Smart Home also offers detailed explanations of the solar

The mkSolaire at MSI surpassed Chicago's green rating system by 50 percent.

panels, wind generation, water catchment, and grey-water systems throughout, and an energy-monitoring system is used to highlight energy consumption.

One of the most rewarding aspects of the "Smart Home: Green + Wired" project is working with the Museum of Science + Industry. The museum is near and dear to my heart because it was such a significant part of my childhood. One day during my middle school years, my eighth-grade class piled into a caravan of buses and drove from Iowa to Chicago to visit this museum. My 300 classmates and I spent the entire day visiting fascinating exhibits like coal mines, railroads, and an accurate reproduction of an old-time "Main Street" with a cobblestone road and gas lamps.

I was also very interested in the museum building itself. The Beaux-Arts masterpiece is the only surviving structure from the 1893 World's Columbian Exposition. I walked through it, amazed and inspired (you just didn't get to see buildings like this in Iowa at that time!). The mixture of grand architecture and science was intoxicating. Immediately after our field trip, I signed up for as many architecture and science classes as I could. Based on my work at MKD, you can see that the mixture of these two interests has clearly persisted in me.

I am enthusiastic about the opportunities the MSI mkSolaire offers to educate and interact with children. Children are the ones motivating us to improve the health of our planet. Children are inspiring to me, so I was thrilled to be working with the museum on this very special project. My biggest hope is

to make the earth a better, healthier place for future generations. Gaining knowledge to make healthy choices and inspiring change, one person at a time, can make a difference.

The ceiling above the main living area stretches from twelve to eighteen
feet high and opens up to the airy loft/library on the second level.

The home's green roof is beautiful
and provides insulation for the roof.

The home uses strategically
designed roofs and windows to
invite light and air into the home.

The living room combines ecological materials, renewable energy systems, smart design, and eco-friendly furnishings.

Walls of glass bring light and breezes inside.

The kitchen, which is situated just off the main living space, is cleverly positioned so that it is not completely visible.

The open plan of the mkSolaire creates a loftlike space that feels big.

The matching mkPure sinks in the master bath were made with fly ash and recycled porcelain.

The mkLotus exhibit in front of San Francisco's City Hall.

*This home was designed as an oasis. We created a house that provides a sense of tranquility. It is about connection—to the landscape and to the natural world.*

## mkLotus

Efficient. Beautiful. Sustainable. We worked hard to ensure the mkLotus embodies the best that green architecture has to offer. First built for a 2007 green conference in San Francisco, our 725-square-foot residence is meant to be a unique haven whose sustainable elements—green roofing system, water catchment system, and recycled building materials—result in a zero-energy bill.

The warm, thoughtful, multifunctional design of the mkLotus, with its slanted wood siding, high ceilings, and skylights, reflects the influence of my hometown in rural Iowa. This modern interpretation of the barn vernacular produces a spacious, healthy, light-filled home with a minimal impact on the environment.

We built the first mkLotus in 2007 as part of the West Coast Green Conference in San Francisco, which every year brings together hundreds of experts and visionaries in the field of sustainable design. One of the main goals of West Coast Green is to inspire people to implement green design in their own homes and to make it easier for homeowners to get the information they need. Situated prominently in front of San Francisco's City Hall, the mkLotus received thousands of visitors during the few days it was on display, many of whom marveled at the fact that such a comfortable home was also environmentally sustainable. *USA Today* commented on the home's "sleek, modern design, lots of windows, and cool, welcoming tones."

For the conference, we built a single-module, one-bedroom version of the mkLotus in eight weeks. The home was shipped in one day and, thanks to the efforts of many committed volunteers, completed on-site in three days. The dedicated efforts of the community resembled an old-fashioned barn-raising and really demonstrated the close connection between sustainability and community. It was amazing to see.

The mkLotus being assembled in front of San Francisco's City Hall.

The clean lines and warm spaces of the mkLotus allow for an eclectic range of choices for the interior. Today, fortunately, an increasing number of designers are creating eco-friendly furnishings. Designed in collaboration with Dan Gregory, senior editor of *Sunset* magazine, the interior of the mkLotus at West Coast Green demonstrated that sustainable design can be both comfortable and beautiful.

Despite its small square footage, the design of the mkLotus ensures a sense of spaciousness. Careful design choices—such as walls composed of accordion glass doors that open to the outdoors, high ceilings, and a sloped roof—nurture a feeling of openness and connection with the natural landscape.

In keeping with our "Smart Design" EcoPrinciple, the mkLotus encourages functional, multiuse spaces. For example, the mkIsland allows homeowners to combine dining and food preparation in one place, and also includes an open-shelving system for kitchen and dining storage. Rather than traditional doors, the mkLotus features sliding screen panels made from recycled plastic that create a sense of openness and flow as you move from one room to another. And the mkVessel, a unique LED entry light also functions as a vase that can hold flowers or other treasured objects.

High-performance insulation, radiant heating, LED lighting fixtures, and solar panels eliminate energy waste, and strategically located skylights and windows nearly eliminate the need for artificial light during the day. The home uses an energy-monitoring system that allows owners to track energy use throughout the day, and it also connects to a state-of-

The mkVessel, a unique LED entry light, also functions as a vase that can hold flowers or other treasured objects.

the-art home theater, audio network, and speaker system. Also, technologies such as dual-flush toilets, low-flow shower-heads and faucets, and on-demand water heaters conserve water, while a green roof system, rainwater catchment system, and grey-water system further limit the home's impact on the water supply. As a result, the mkLotus home exceeds the Green Point Rating System by 300 percent.

Beauty and sustainability continue outside the walls of the mkLotus home too. For the West Coast Green Conference in San Francisco, the landscape design featured a series of separate outdoor "rooms," each of which made use of drought-tolerant plants. Well-designed sustainable outdoor spaces add considerable livable square footage to a home, and can include patios, decks, outdoor bathrooms, and outdoor kitchens. All of these options offer a way to connect to the natural world without increasing a home's impact on the environment.

The 100 percent sustainable garden, designed by Nicholas Thayer of Late Afternoon Garden Design, included reused and recycled products whenever possible. On-site water retention was accomplished with permeable paving and plantings. A bioswale of native sedges extended the function of the green roof to collect and filter water and return it to the ground. In addition to water conservation, the use of native and adaptive plants created a sense of place and connection with nature. Thoughtful landscaping can be restorative as well as sustainable. One day after the mkLotus garden was planted, local hummingbirds came to feed on the autumn sage and verbenas.

Careful design choices, such as accordion glass walls, nurture a feeling of openness and connection with the natural landscape.

The rainwater catchment system doubles as a lovely water feature in the garden.

Beauty and sustainability continue outside the walls of the mkLotus home too.

Concrete countertops and FSC-certified cabinetry.

The light-filled mkLotus bedroom.

Eco-friendly closet doors add plenty of storage.

Functional multiuse spaces make the 725-square-foot home feel spacious.

Nicholas Thayer's thoughtful landscaping plan ensured watering was kept to a minimum.

The warm materials and generous natural sunlight in an Aspen custom home.

*Sustainability isn't just about the way we build. It is a state of mind. We want to design homes that embody and nurture that state of mind.*

## mkCustom

For many people, the word *prefab* suggests standardized structures that might be functional but are unlikely to express a distinct personality. This couldn't be further from the truth. With mkCustom, we make the most of our experience with modular technology and sustainable materials to craft homes to suit individual tastes and family needs while responding creatively to varying landscapes. Our designs allow a great deal of flexibility so that clients can easily tailor a house to accommodate a difficult site, make the most of a view, add a studio, or integrate a carport, for example. There is nothing cookie-cutter about these custom homes. In ways large and small, we merge design solutions and green modular technology to create appealing homes whose features express the unique sensibilities of their owners.

Our biggest goal was to create a light-filled home that felt spacious despite its small footprint.

## Aspen, Colorado, Home

Nestled in the Elk Mountains of the Rockies, Aspen is one of the most charming and scenic ski towns in the country. But sometimes even a beautiful building site can be tricky. A custom home in Aspen, Colorado, presented us with the challenge of designing a family home only thirteen feet high and within serious setback constraints.

We had a small area on which to build, so it really put our first EcoPrinciple, "Smart Design," to the test. Our biggest goal was to create a light-filled home that felt spacious despite its small footprint. In order to provide necessary space, we carefully excavated to create a lower level with a lovely adjacent garden. We also extended the living spaces beyond the home's actual walls with large folding glass doors. These transparent boundaries, used on two sides of the living area, dissolve the corners and connect to the scenic outdoors. Outdoor rooms expand the usable space to create a feeling of openness. As a result, the gathering areas feel much larger than they really are.

The open plan creates a distinct communal area for gathering, eating, and living, allowing the kitchen to become the true heart of the home. The multifunctional kitchen includes an information/entertainment center as well as a large L-shaped island used as a family gathering and discussion area during meal preparation. Warm bamboo cabinetry blends with bamboo wood floors so the gathering space feels like a cohesive piece of well-designed living

146

An elegant curve in the roofline also accommodates the snow load.

casework. Creative details like a back-painted glass back-splash add a personal touch.

Naturally, we wanted to capture the gorgeous mountain views surrounding the site. To that end, we designed "pop-up" roofs with high triangular-shaped windows to bring the views in. These windows also allow the sun to wash the ceiling with light during the day, eliminating the need to turn on lights in daylight hours.

Snow loads always need to be considered when designing in places like Colorado. For this custom home, we increased the wood-framing size and decreased the spacing from a typical home. We also decided to introduce an elegant curve into the roofline to accommodate the snow load yet maintain a roomy ceiling height.

The living spaces extend beyond the home's actual walls with large folding glass doors.

The open plan creates a distinct communal area for gathering, eating, and living, allowing the kitchen to become the true heart of the home.

## Southern California Beach House

This Southern California weekend home for a family and their visiting friends needed to accommodate large groups yet keep its overall size in check. To accomplish this, we designed the home with an open, airy lower floor plan. Large doors can be opened to create gathering spaces or closed off for cozier private rooms.

The ocean view is captured by a wall of glass accordion doors that can completely open to the outdoors, and the master suite includes an outdoor deck that extends both the bedroom and bathroom to the outside. The entire master suite can be opened up to the ocean view to create a complete indoor/outdoor experience.

mkCustom

## New Camaldoli Hermitage Monastery

The New Camaldoli Hermitage Monastery complex, located on a breathtaking bluff overlooking the ocean in Big Sur, California, was comprised of failing structures built with volunteer labor and a very limited budget. Originally built in 1958 (before building codes), the campus was plagued by unhealthy mold, termite damage, and low-quality materials.

We designed a large community master plan to include an infirmary, workers quarters, bookstore, retreat center, monks' cells, formation center, dining room, library, and multipurpose building. When complete, this new complex will become a peaceful retreat, blending seamlessly into the natural surroundings and leaving little negative impact on the environment.

The goal is to create a peaceful retreat that blends seamlessly into the natural surroundings with little negative impact on the environment.

The home revolves around the center hearth space, a unique fireplace/ cabinetry design that circulates up the three stories of the home.

This custom Santa Barbara home features green amenities such as a water catchment system and saline pool.

The Santa Barbara sun powers the home's solar panels, while doors and windows promote cross-breezes throughout the home.

The new mkHearth is inspired by rural structures in the American landscape.

Double-paned glass folding doors and a barn-door sunscreen on this mkSolaire allow residents to regulate sunlight and temperature naturally.

*"Design for sustainability means fostering innovation—not just in products and services but in work methods, behaviors, and business practices."*

—JOHN THACKARA, *ETERNALLY YOURS*, 1998

## What's Next?

As we look ahead to the future, it is inspiring to realize that an increasing number of people agree: green is good. A generation ago, if the public thought about green design at all, they imagined geodesic domes with space-age windows. But as awareness of ecological issues has increased, so have the questions we ask about how and where we live. How are our homes constructed? Is there lead in the paint we use? How can we reduce waste and conserve energy in our homes? Many of our current buildings are making us sick. What is the cost of our health? How does this translate into how we design and build? We have a marvelous opportunity to rethink the way we build and the way we live. Sustainable living is no longer merely the concern of a few; it can now be a healthy lifestyle for many.

In a remarkably short period of time, green has gone mainstream. The last few years have been pivotal not only for green building but also for the green movement in general. People are becoming more engaged with ecological issues and more willing to do what they can to protect our natural resources and to improve our built environments. Magazines feature "green issues" that highlight developments in organic foods, hybrid cars, and solar panels. Celebrities tout the latest environmentally friendly products.

The contemporary movement for sustainable living has a powerful ally in technology. The cycle of innovation in alternative energy is now very short, for example. Products and systems using renewable and recyclable materials and energy are everywhere. Stores now feature hundreds of new green-building products, from recycled plastic decking to nontoxic paints and textiles. Green expos and trade shows are thriving. And American consumers are demanding sustainable, responsible products.

These new products and technologies have helped to challenge the "bigger is better" philosophy that has been a hallmark of American consumerism for so long. Take, for example, the popular Apple iPhone. When this little gadget hit the market, it proved that cell phones were no longer just for making calls. Today, technology must be multifunctional—so the iPhone includes a camera, an mp3 player, a photo gallery, and a means for checking e-mail and surfing the Internet. As avid iPhone users demonstrated, a bigger phone wasn't the answer—a better phone was. This paradigm shift—away from

The Sunset Breezehouse kitchen is comprised entirely of environmentally responsible materials and energy-efficient appliances.

"bigger is better" to multifunctional—has reached far beyond devices like cell phones. It is now part of a broader cultural conversation about how to do more with less.

We all know that during their construction and life cycle, buildings consume huge amounts of the earth's resources. The United States Green Building Council (USGBC) notes that buildings account for more than one-third of carbon emissions in the United States and consume 70 percent of the electricity load. By 2015, the USGBC estimates that fifteen million new buildings will have been constructed in the United States. We should see this kind of growth as an opportunity to improve our design and construction practices. Sustainability isn't a luxury; it's now a requirement for responsible growth as we move into the future.

But what, exactly, does it mean to live "green"? How do we know if the product we buy or the house we live in is environmentally responsible? There is now a certification process for products seeking a "green" label. Energy Star, a joint program of the U.S. Environmental Protection Agency and the U.S. Department of Energy, certifies that products meet strict energy guidelines, save money, and protect the environment. In addition, the Forest Stewardship Council (FSC) promotes global forest management with its rigorous standards. The FSC in the United States is recognized by fourteen environmental organizations and major businesses.

For homes, there are several ratings programs available that clarify what is and isn't green in a home's features.

Relaxing in a Breezehouse library.

Independent ratings sources—most notably Leadership in Energy and Environmental Design (LEED) for Homes, which launched in 2007—provide independent third-party verification that a building project meets the highest green building and performance measures. In addition, the NAHB (National Association of Home Builders) will soon be unveiling a new Green Globes rating classification as an alternative to the standard LEED system.

Local green-building programs can have even more relevancy. Unlike national codes and ratings programs that are not able to call out regional nuances, local programs can address specific climates and conditions. For example, what

Green design strategies (like this double-pane glass accordion door, which enlarges the living area and invites in natural light and breezes) are a natural fit with multifamily housing.

might be considered sustainable building in New York or Alaska might not be suitable for New Mexico.

## Green Multifamily: Meaningful Communities

As environmental concerns continue to mount, developers are beginning to recognize the many benefits of sustainable prefabricated architecture. Shorter time frames for construction, predictable costs, government incentives, and lowered risk and liability are only a few of the benefits of integrating sustainable practices and products into our built environments. We believe that green design strategies are a natural fit with multifamily housing, and now larger developers are beginning to follow in the footsteps of smaller design-build companies. Through the use of smart sustainable design and site strategies, energy-efficient systems, and eco-friendly materials, we can create low-impact communities that are healthy, beautiful, and cost effective.

As we have seen, homes and the land they use have big effects on the environment, human health, and local communities. Sustainable development is a more holistic approach to creating healthier, more environmentally responsible neighborhoods. Instead of concentrating on individual components of sustainability, we consider the whole system. If we incorporate alternative-energy systems like solar or geothermal power, we can potentially reinvest the energy savings back into the community in the form of organic gardens, exercise facilities, and other beneficial additions. And, in terms of sustainability, multifamily housing has single-family homes

158

Sustainable development is a more holistic approach to creating healthier, more environmentally responsible neighborhoods.

The SolTerra multifamily project.

beat. Multifamily communities are more energy efficient, use less land, and are often more pedestrian-friendly with easier access to public transportation (no car needed).

SolTerra is a twenty-four-unit multifamily project we have recently completed in San Leandro, California. This collection of homes is dotted with communal and private gardens and utilizes sustainable materials and methods, high-end finishes, and private garages. Each unit is a two-bedroom, two-bath home, with a bonus/lounge/office space and offers high-performance insulation, mechanical systems, and solar power to offset energy costs.

We are also working with a highly respected value-based development group in Denver on a few environmentally friendly multifamily projects. One project will consist of a forty-unit town house development with a mix of two- and three-bedroom, two-story homes at both affordable and market rates. This community will include shared parks, communal organic gardens, geothermal alternative energy sources, high-performance energy systems, and beautiful sustainable

The Denver community project will include parks, organic gardens, and alternative energy sources.

An mkHearth community.

materials and strategies. This financially and socially blended community will share the same goal of living a healthy lifestyle in green homes.

To accommodate dense urban environments, we have also started to focus on neighborhood infill projects. We hope to knit together existing neighborhoods with healthy green housing.

My hope for the future is an industry where green practices are so accepted and pervasive that the "green" label will not be a necessary qualifier—it will simply be the way we build and the way we live. Just as child-safety seats and seat belts are now considered a necessity for your car, I hope designing and building a home in a thoughtful sustainable manner will be the norm. In addition to homeowners asking "how much" a green product or home will cost, I hope they will frequently ask what the product is made of, where it came from, and

how it will impact the environment. In the future, we hope to see more and more homeowners embracing the philosophy of green design and living.

Another hope is to make green building even more affordable, and I look forward to changes in the way homeowners view the cost of building green. Costs should not be only confined to the purchase price (up-front cost). We should be primarily concerned about our monthly bill and long-term costs associated with owning and maintaining a residence. When we evaluate a home's cost in this way, green buildings cost less than non-green buildings.

Another dream of mine is to see a change in the way real estate agents list homes on the market. A description relating the size, price, and number of bedrooms is not adequate anymore. Homes could be listed with labels, like foods, to

We need to make these goals simpler for people to achieve by providing easy off-the-shelf solutions that make use of green technology to produce those necessary objects of daily life.

Sustainability is not just a hip or trendy notion; it's an obligation not just for ourselves but for future generations. The future presents us with unique challenges and numerous opportunities to redesign our built environment. As an architect, I believe that even the small changes we make in our daily lives—as well as the large decisions we make about the kinds of homes we want to live in—can make a difference. We can all let the green in.

We also focus on infill projects to accommodate dense urban environments.

highlight anticipated energy and water usage for the home. Perhaps materials are called out, and calculated numbers can tell you how much off-gassing and toxins you can expect in your space. For an asthmatic child or a chemically sensitive adult, this could be a wonderful resource.

We are enthusiastic about the expanding marketplace for green goods that answer consumer needs while respecting the principles of sustainability. In addition to our work on multifamily housing, our aim is to develop green products and design systems that are both affordable and easily integrated into daily life. People want lower energy bills and lower water bills, and they want a healthy environment for their families.

# Acknowledgments

We would like to thank the many wonderful individuals who have made significant contributions to our work. We feel so fortunate to be supported by an amazing group of visionaries, writers, designers, builders, sustainable leaders, and friends. Many special thanks to Dan Gregory, Beth Whiteley, Peter Whiteley, Shannon Thompson, Katie Tamony, and everyone at *Sunset* magazine; Christopher Hawthorne, Alana Stang, Reed Haslach, Donald Albrecht, Lisa Grossman, Hank Grifith, Cathy Frankel, and everyone at the National Building Museum; David Mosena, Kurt Haunfelner, Anne Rashford, Jeff Johnson, Jim Marshall, JB Spector, Steven Beaseley, Norcon, and everyone at the Museum of Science + Industry; Christi Graham and everyone at West Coast Green; Allison Arieff, Bryan Burkhart, Michael Sylvester, Dwell Magazine, WIRED Magazine, Ellen Rockne, Brian Andreas, Jim Thompson, John Swain, Glen Haney, Wing Yu, Kim and Conie Remick, Scott and Jenna Komoto, Todd and Katie Gardner, Andrew and Kindra Reid, Nancy and Arn Tellem, Richard and Brancy McAniff, Sylvia White, Marty Moore, and the entire AddSpace family; Petes Towing, Jodi Schiller and Ben Douglas, Bill Orrick, Marv Shetler, and the fabulous team at Blazer; Rick Bartolotti, Kevin George, Paul Melish, Sue Powers, Sarah Doody, Barry Reder, Merritt Sher, Peter Lui, Sim Van Der Ryn, Nicholas Thayer, Marshall Mayer, Alex Hinds, Maya Draisin, Mike Freed, Fred and Micholyn Brown, Jack and Mary Ann Remick, John Holt, Todd Lash, Joe Marshall, Joe Glorfield, Mark Finser, Ben Black, Josh Becker, Eric Whitaker, Bob Epstein, Cynthia Ringo, Bill Green, Barry Traub, Taylor Robinson, Sadia Harper, Mary and Jon Kaufmann, Rev. Raniero Hoffman, F. Michael Fish, Br. Michael Harrington, Andrew Rifkin, Melissa Doering, Ted Fentin, Steven Addis, Marlou Rodriquez, Martin Waibel, Deborah Marshall, Isabelle Remick, Pam and Lou Stolba, Cynthia Stolba, Jeffrey, Hugo and Sebastian Rosen, Christine and John Foley, Ann and Justin Lumley, the Sullivans, all the Remicks near and far, the Tomas, the Inhouses, the Devereaux, the Kaune-Smiths, the Orrs, the Williams, the Sova-Carters, Wayne and Judy Eckstien, Patti Hall, and Michael French.

We feel particularly fortunate to be working with a talented and dedicated group of people including Kevin Cullen, Joseph Remick, Scott Landry, Dick Hawkinson, Paul Warner, Lisa Gansky, John Mick, Chris Downey, Mike Brown, James Kean, Jason Kohler, Andrew Faust, Justin Brown, Verl Adams, Tuanh Ta, Cristina Perdomo, Rebecca Woelke, Kevin Smeds, Jamileh Cannon, Jim Glossner, Larry Miller, Dorothy Caudill, Virginia Sledjeski-Rae, Fred Rae, Jessica Choi, Amber Riley, Donn Fleming, Eric Irvine, Shane Stanbro, Karen Baik, Emanuele Naboni, Courtney Cruz, Levi Conover, Stephen Rice, Dennise Morrison, Christopher Peak, Bret Harrell, Darren Ray, Doug Griffith, Kelly Fitzpatrick, and Lynn DeTienne.

A very special thanks to Christine Rosen and Kelly Melia-Teevan for contributing to the book with writing, editing, coordination, and endless cheerleading, and to Gibbs Smith and editor Hollie Keith for all their hard work on this book.

A heartfelt thank-you to all our friends and family.

# Glossary

**alternative energy:** Energy from a source other than fossil-fuel sources of oil, natural gas, and coal (i.e., wind, running water, the sun).

**biodegradable:** Capable of decomposing under natural conditions.

**bioswale:** A system that uses plants and soil and/or compost to hold and cleanse runoff from a site, roadway, or other source.

**building envelope:** The exterior of a building's construction—the walls, windows, floors, roof, and floor.

**button-up:** The process where set mods are bolted down and finished.

**carbon footprint:** A measure of the quantity of carbon dioxide expended through the burning of fossil fuels. A carbon footprint is usually referred to in tons of carbon dioxide or tons of carbon emitted, and provides a means for measuring the impact of human activity on the planet.

**cellulose insulation:** An alternative insulation to glass fiber insulation. Cellulose insulation is usually a mix of waste paper and fire retardant, and has thermal properties superior to glass fiber. Glass fiber batt insulation often contains formaldehyde, which can adversely affect indoor air quality and human health, and the glass fibers themselves are hazardous if inhaled and irritating to the skin and eyes. Certain cellulose insulations can have a high recycled content for maximum environmental benefit.

**compact fluorescent lamp (CFL):** Small fluorescent lamps used as more energy-efficient alternatives to incandescent lighting. CFLs use less power and have a longer-rated life span.

**construction waste:** Waste building materials, landscape debris, and rubble resulting from construction, remodeling, repair, and demolition of homes, commercial buildings, and other structures and pavements. Certain components of construction waste can contain lead, asbestos, or other hazardous substances.

**daylighting:** The use of natural light in an interior space to substitute for artificial light. Daylighting is considered a sustainable building strategy because it reduces energy use and (when well-designed) can maximize visual comfort and productivity.

**demand hot water system:** These are hot water heaters designed to provide instantaneous hot water, rather than storing preheated hot water in a tank. These hot water systems can serve an entire home or be "point-of-use." Benefits include less energy and water waste.

**eco-friendly:** Little or no impact on a native ecosystem.

**Energy Star:** A program administered by the Environmental Protection Agency that evaluates products based on energy efficiency.

**engineered lumber/wood:** Composite wood products made from lumber, fiber, sawdust, and glue. Engineered wood products can be environmentally preferable to dimensional lumber, because they waste wood and small-diameter trees to produce structural building materials. Engineered wood products can be stronger and less prone to warping from humidity than typical lumber.

**fly ash:** Substitution of fly ash for portland cement in concrete is considered a sustainable building strategy, as it reduces the amount of energy-intensive (and $CO_2$-producing) cement in the mix. Fly ash also provides performance enhancements such as a denser, smoother, and more detailed finish than traditional concrete.

**Forest Stewardship Council (FSC):** A third-party certification organization that evaluates the sustainability of forest products. FSC-certified wood products have met detailed criteria in areas such as forest management, worker conditions, and fair trade.

**formaldehyde:** A colorless irritating gas, CH20, used primarily as a disinfectant and preservative and in producing other compounds like resins.

**geothermal/ground source heat pump:** These heat pumps use underground coils to transfer heat from the naturally more stable temperature of the earth to the inside of a building. This type of heat pump provides substantial energy savings over conventional heat pumps.

**global warming:** An increase in the global mean temperature of the earth that is widely believed to be a result of increased emissions of greenhouse gases trapped in the atmosphere.

**grey water:** Domestic wastewater composed of wash water from kitchen, bathroom, and laundry sinks, tubs, and washers.

**grey water reuse:** A strategy for reducing wastewater; diverts the gray water to productive uses such as underground irrigation and non-potable functions such as toilet flushing.

**green:** A widely used term to describe buildings or products designed and constructed with minimal negative impact to the environment. Green building and manufacturing can utilize renewable, raw, and recycled materials or energy sources but emphasizes the conservation of resources, energy efficiency, and healthful interior spaces.

**green roof:** A planted green space on a building roof. Green roofs maintain living plants on top of a membrane and drainage system. Green roofs are considered a sustainable building strategy because they can reduce stormwater runoff from a site and modulate temperatures in and around the building. Green roofs also have thermal-insulating properties and can provide habitat for wildlife and open space for humans.

**greenwash:** A term used to describe disinformation distributed by a person or an organization in order to present an environmentally responsible public image.

**high efficiency:** A general term for technologies and processes that require less energy, water, or other inputs to operate. A goal in sustainable building is to achieve high efficiency in resource use when compared to a conventional practice.

**indoor air quality (IAQ):** The American Society of Heating, Refrigerating and Air Conditioning Engineers (ASHRAE) defines acceptable indoor air quality as air in which there are no known contaminants at harmful concentrations. IAQ can be affected by microbial contaminants such as mold, or bacteria, chemicals, or allergens. Ventilation to dilute indoor contaminants is a way of improving IAQ.

**kit house:** A home that is comprised of prefabricated parts, delivered, and then assembled on the site.

**LEED:** A self-assessing green-building rating system developed by the U.S. Green Building Council. LEED stands for Leadership in Energy and Environmental Design, and evaluates a building from a systems perspective. By achieving points in different areas of environmental performance, a building achieves a level of "certification" under the system.

**life cycle:** All stages of a product's development, from extraction of fuel for power to production, marketing, use, and disposal.

**light-emitting diode (LED):** A long-lasting illumination technology used for many different applications, including residential lighting. One of the key advantages of LED-based lighting is its high efficiency.

**low-emissivity (low-e) windows:** Window technology that lowers the amount of energy loss through windows by preventing the transmission of radiant heat while still allowing adequate light to pass through.

**manufactured home:** A home built on a trailer chassis and manufactured off-site using lightweight metal framing; it must meet HUD code requirements.

**marriage lines:** The area where two mods come together.

**mobile home:** A manufactured home made prior to 1976 and considered portable and temporary.

**modular home:** A highly engineered home built in an off-site facility in modules or sections and then delivered to the intended site of use. The modules are assembled using either a crane or trucks.

**natural ventilation:** Ventilation design that uses existing breezes on a site and natural convection to move and distribute air through a building or space. Strategies can include placement of operable windows and doors, thermal chimneys, landscape berms to direct airflow on a site, and operable skylights.

**nonrenewable:** Refers to a material as well as an energy source. A nonrenewable resource uses materials or energy that, once used, are gone forever and cannot be renewed through natural processes. Examples would include certain species of wood, some minerals (for materials), and petroleum and natural gas (for energy sources).

**off-gassing:** The release of volatile chemicals from a product or assembly. Many chemicals released from materials (such as carpeting) impact indoor air quality and occupant health.

**panelized system:** A system including wall, roof, and floor sections/panels that are made in a factory instead of on a construction site; SIPs are an example of a panelized system.

**passive solar:** An approach for using the sun's energy to heat (or cool) a space, mass, or liquid. Passive solar uses no pumps or mechanical controls to function. A solarium is an example of a passive solar technique.

**prefab home:** A dwelling constructed off-site, usually in standard sections and then shipped to a site.

**radiant heat:** Heat transferred in the form of light energy. The radiant heat energy is emitted from a warm element (floor, wall, overhead panel) and warms people and other objects in rooms rather than directly heating the air. Radiant heat allows the air temperature of a room to be lower, yet occupants remain at a comfortable temperature.

**rainwater catchment/harvest:** Rainwater harvest and storage systems captured and used on-site to offset drinkable water needs for a building and/or landscape. Many different systems exist, but most consist of a surface for collecting precipitation (roof or other impervious surface) and a storage system (cistern). Depending on the end use, a variety of filtering and purifying systems may also be used.

**reclaimed:** Reclaimed materials are similar to recycled products because they have been diverted from waste to be used for something else. An example would be reclaimed lumber, taken from an old building and refurbished for a new purpose.

**recyclable:** A recyclable material can be reused again and again in the making of another product.

**recycled:** Collecting, separating, and processing a material that might otherwise end up in a landfill. A recycled material contains some percentage of these recovered materials in the finished product.

**set:** The action of removing the mods from their transportation onto the site foundation, usually via crane.

**SIPs:** This is the acronym for "structural insulated panels," a factory-made panelized system used to replace standard stick framing and usually created by sandwiching a thick layer of foam (polystyrene or polyurethane) between two layers of Oriented Strand Board (OSB), plywood, or fiber-cement.

**solar panels:** General term for an assembly of photovoltaic (PV) modules. Using solar panels is a sustainable building strategy that reduces a building's dependence on nonrenewable sources of power distributed through the grid system.

**stack effect:** Air, as in a chimney, that moves upward because it is warmer than the ambient atmosphere.

**stick built:** A home built using conventional methods entirely on-site; also called site-built.

**sunshades:** Devices for blocking unwanted sunlight and solar heat gain.

**sustainable:** The concept of sustainability can be traced back to President Theodore Roosevelt, who stated in 1910: "I recognize the right and duty of this generation to develop and use the natural resources of our land; but I do not recognize the right to waste them, or to rob, by wasteful use, the generations that come after us." Sustainable materials and development should, in theory, last indefinitely, without compromising the resources of the future. Sustainable products and materials are those that decrease their environmental impact at each stage of their life cycle.

**thermal mass:** A mass (such as stone, concrete, or brick) used to store heat. When used correctly in a building, it can be a useful technique for controlling the flow or storage of heat for occupant comfort.

**ventilation:** The deliberate movement of air outside a building to the inside.

**volatile organic compound (VOC)**: Organic compounds that fade away at room temperatures, cause poor indoor air quality, and are dangerous to human health. Sources of VOCs include solvents and paints. Many materials commonly used in traditional building construction such as adhesives, carpets, furniture, and paints emit VOCs.

**wastewater:** The spent or used water from a home, community, farm, or industry that contains dissolved or suspended matter.

**wind turbine:** A device for converting the kinetic energy of the wind into electricity.

## Credits and Resources

**Chapter 1: Dreaming of Green**

Photography: Michelle Kaufmann and John Swain
  Photography

**Chapter 2: Thoughtful, Sustainable Design for Everyone**

Eames photos by Eames Demetrios © 2000 Eames Office, LLC
  (www.eamesoffice.com)

Eichler photos by Ernie Braun

**Chapter 3: The 5 EcoPrinciples**

Photography: John Swain Photography and Nick Gunderson

Energy Study: Emanuele Naboni

**Chapter 4: Green Prefab**

Photography: Michelle Kaufmann, All American Homes, and
  John Swain Photography

## Chapter 5: Glidehouse

*Kaufmann-Cullen Glidehouse*

Designers: Michelle Kaufmann, Kevin Cullen

Builder: Cullen Fine Woodworking, Rob Arge

Photographers: Michelle Kaufmann and John Swain
    Photography

*Sunset Glidehouse*

Designers: Michelle Kaufmann, Peter O. Whiteley / *Sunset*,
    Dan Gregory / *Sunset*, Dick Hawkinson / MKD

Engineer: Martin Weibel

Builder: CRG, Britco

Photographers: Tom Story / Sunset Publishing Co. and JMC
    Photography

*Reid Glidehouse*

Designers: Michelle Kaufmann, Dick Hawkinson, MKD,
    Kindra Reid

Owner-Engineer: Martin Wiebel

Builder: CRG, Britco

Photographer: Nick Gunderson

*Walker / McElroy Glidehouse*

Designers: Michelle Kaufmann, Dick Hawkinson / MKD; Ami
    McElroy

Engineer: Martin Weibel

Builder: CRG, Blazer

Photographer: Mike Jensen

*Remick Glidehouse*

Designers: Michelle Kaufmann, Scott Landry / MKD; Conie +
    Kim Remick

Engineer: Martin Weibel

Builder: Walden

Landscape Design: Nick Thayer / Late Afternoon Design

Photographer: John Swain Photography

## Chapter 6: Sunset Breezehouse

*Sunset Breezehouse at Sunset*

Designers: Michelle Kaufmann, Scott Landry, Paul Warner,
    Dick Hawkinson / MKD; Dan Gregory, Peter O. Whiteley /
    *Sunset* magazine

Engineer: Martin Wiebel / Canstruct Engineering Group

Builder: Britco, CRG, DeMattei Construction, RCA Construction,
    Cullen Fine Woodworking

Photographer: Tom Story / Sunset Publishing Co.

*Komoto Sunset Breezehouse*

Designers: Michelle Kaufmann, Scott Landry, Dick Hawkinson,
    MKD

Engineer: Ralph Tavares / R&S Tavares Associates

Builder: Robert Brown Construction, Inc., Britco

Landscape Design: Joni Janecki

Photographer: John Swain Photography

*Rockne-Andreas Custom Sunset Breezehouse*

Designers: Michelle Kaufmann, Scott Landry, Paul Warner,
    Dick Hawkinson / MKD; Ellen Rockne

Engineer: Martin Wiebel / Canstruct Engineering Group

Builder: mkConstructs, and Dennis Allen+ Associates

Landscape Design: Margie Grace

Photographer: John Swain Photography


*Haney-Yu Sunset Breezehouse*

Designers: Michelle Kaufmann, Scott Landry, Dick Hawkinson
Levi Conover / MKD

Engineer: Martin Wiebel / Canstruct Engineering Group

Builder: mkConstructs and Paul Melish Builders

Landscape Design: Glen Haney

Photographers: John Swain Photography and Rachel Styer


*Dry Creek Valley Sunset Breezehouse, Sonoma County, California*

Designers: Michelle Kaufmann, Scott Landry, Paul Warner,
Joseph Remick, Dick Hawkinson / MKD

Interiors: Steven Miller

Landscape Design: Deakin and Vanozzi

Builder: mkConstructs and Steven Murray

Photographer: John Swain Photography


## Chapter 7: mkSolaire

Museum of Science and Industry mkSolaire / Smart Home:
Green and Wired exhibit

Designers: Michelle Kaufmann, Scott Landry, Levi Conover /
MKD, Jeffrey Johnson (MSI)

Engineer: Tylk Gustafson Reckers Wilson Andrews, LLC

Builder: All American and Norcon

Landscape Design: University of Illinois Extension

Photographers: All American Homes, Michelle Kaufmann,
John Swain Photography, J. B. Spector / MSI


## Chapter 8: mkLotus

Designers: Michelle Kaufmann, James Kean, Scott Landry,
Levi Conover / MKD

Interiors: Dan Gregory / *Sunset* magazine, Cristina Perdomo,
Rebecca Woelke / MKD

West Coast Green Team: Christi Graham, Karen Jackson,
Abby Kojola

Landscape Design: Nick Thayer / Late Afternoon Design

Builder: Eric Peterson / Altamont Homes; Reed Walker / Mod-
Tech; and Todd Lukesh, Ronald Yen and Phil Williams /
Webcor

Photographer: John Swain Photography


## Chapter 9: mkCustom

*Aspen, Colorado Home*

Designers: Paul Warner, Michelle Kaufmann, Dick Hawkinson
/ MKD

Structural: Martin Wiebel / Canstruct Engineering Group

Factory: mkConstructs and Mark Hesselschwerdt / Buckaroo
Builders

Landscape Design: Joni Janecki

Photographer: Jim Thompson


*Southern California Beach House*

Designers: Michelle Kaufmann, Stephen Rice, Tuanh Ta, Lynn
Detienne, Scott Landry, Andrew Faust, MKD

Interiors: Thierry Marchand


*New Camaldoli Hermitage Monastery*

Designers: Michelle Kaufmann, Stephen Rice, Scott Landry / MKD

**Chapter 10: Where are We Headed?**

Photography: Sunset Publishing Co., John Swain Photography,
   Cutter Cutshaw

Author Jacket Photos:

Michelle Kaufmann by Cutter Cutshaw

Catherine Remick by Terry Riggins

## References

Arieff, A., "The Proof Is in the Prefab," *Dwell,* November 2004.

Braungart, Michael, and William McDonough. *Cradle to Cradle: Remaking the Way We Make Things.* New York: North Point Press, 2002.

Building Performance Report: Hurricane Andrew in Florida, FIA-22, Item 3-0180 (obtained from www.bobvila.com, "Modular homes make sense, January 2008**).**

Eames Office Resources: www.eamesoffice.com

Eichler Network, "Unfolding the Eichler Design": http://www.eichlernetwork.com/ENStory7.html

Energy Star: www.energystar.gov/

Environmental Protection Agency: www.epa.gov

Freed, Eric Corey. *Green Building and Remodeling for Dummies.* Hoboken, NJ: Wiley Publishing, Inc., 2008.

Gregory, D. "Meet the Glidehouse, a Modern Prefab," *Sunset,* 2004.

Katz, Peter. *The New Urbanism: Towards an Architecture of Community.* New York: McGraw-Hill, 1994.

Kennedy, L. "Gliding Along," *Seattle Homes and Lifestyles,* November 2005.

The Museum of Science and Industry:
www.msichicago.org

National Association of Home Builders. NAHB model green building home building guidelines. Washington, D.C.: National Association of Home Builders, 2006.

*New York Post.* "It's a Fab, Fab World," October 4, 2007.

*New York Times.* "As Told to Bethany Lyttle," October 10, 2004.

Olsson, Karen. "Prefabs with Modernist Sensibility," *New York Times,* February 15, 2006.

*San Francisco Chronicle.* "A Model House for the Modern Age: Sunset Magazine Showcases Its New Kid on the Block," May 19, 2005.

Sears Archives:
http://www.searsarchives.com/

Seattle City Green Building:
http://www.seattle.gov/dpd/GreenBuilding/OurProgram/Resources/Greenbuildingglossary/default.asp#F

Scheckel, Paul. *The Home Energy Diet: How to Save Money by Making Your House Energy Smart.* British Colombia, Canada: New Society Publishers, 2005.

www.Skyscraper.org

Stoyke, Godo. *The Carbon Buster's Home Energy Handbook: Slowing Climate Change and Saving Money.* British Colombia, Canada: New Society Publishers, 2007.

*USA Today.* "Green Construction Guidelines Go Residential," September 20, 2007.

U.S. Department of Energy:
http://www.energy.gov/

U.S. Green Building Council. LEED-NC v2.2 reference guide. Washington, D.C.: U.S. Green Building Council, 2005.

U.S. Library of Congress, "The Work of Charles and Ray Eames": www.loc.gov/exhibits/eames/space.html

Walker Art Museum. "Some Assembly Required": http://design.walkerart.org/prefab/Main/PrefabEssay

Whiteley, P. "The Sunset Breezehouse." *Sunset,* May 2005.

174